THE MAS

"Like a Balenciaga suit designed ⸻ ⸺ ⸺ ⸺ the body rather than hug it, Blume's artful blend of history, reporting, and chat conjures the designer's world . . ."
—Rhonda Lieberman, *Bookforum*

"A wonderful, downright romantic story told in as much detail as we'll probably ever see."   —Blouin Artinfo

"An intimate view of a man so few knew about."
—*The Economist*

"Fresh . . . Blume's needle's-eye portrait nearly supports Hubert de Givenchy's conviction that his mentor was 'a perfect man.'"   —Amy Fine Collins, *Vanity Fair*

"Remarkable . . . Blume lends validity to an otherwise elusive history."   —*V Magazine*

"Mary Blume unveils the private world of one of fashion's most reclusive geniuses, Cristóbal Balenciaga, who famously never gave an interview and remained a mystery to even his most devoted clients."   —*WSJ. Magazine*

"[An] intimate, enthusiastic, and lively first biography of the enigmatic designer . . . [Blume] writes with wit and aplomb."   —*Publishers Weekly*

MARY BLUME
THE MASTER OF US ALL

Mary Blume, a native New Yorker who lives in Paris, was a longtime columnist for the *International Herald Tribune*. She is the author of *Côte d'Azur: Inventing the French Riviera* and of a collection of her *Herald Tribune* pieces, *A French Affair*.

ALSO BY MARY BLUME

Côte d'Azur: Inventing the French Riviera

A French Affair: The Paris Beat, 1965–1998

THE MASTER
OF US ALL

THE MASTER

MARY BLUME

FARRAR · STRAUS · GIROUX   NEW YORK

OF US ALL

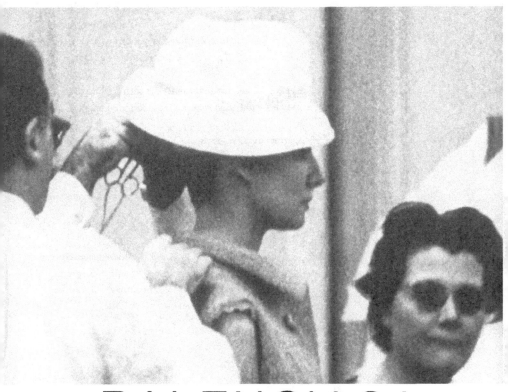

BALENCIAGA,

HIS WORKROOMS,

HIS WORLD

Farrar, Straus and Giroux
18 West 18th Street, New York 10011

Published in 2013 by Farrar, Straus and Giroux
First paperback edition, 2014

The Library of Congress has cataloged the hardcover edition as follows:
Blume, Mary.
The master of us all : Balenciaga, his workrooms, his world /
Mary Blume. — First edition.
    pages   cm
Includes bibliographical references.
ISBN 978-0-374-29873-9 (hardback)
    1. Balenciaga, Cristóbal, 1895–1972.   2. Fashion designers—
France—Biography.   3. Fashion designers—Spain—Biography.
4. Fashion design—Spain—History—20th century.   5. Fashion
design—France—History—20th century.   I. Title.

TT505.B28 B59 2013
746.9'2092—dc23
[B]

                                                        2012029933

Paperback ISBN: 978-0-374-53438-7

Designed by Jonathan D. Lippincott

www.fsgbooks.com
www.twitter.com/fsgbooks • www.facebook.com/fsgbooks

For Thea and Al

Style? A certain lightness. A sense of shame excluding certain actions or reactions. A certain proposition of elegance. The supposition that, despite everything, a melody can be looked for and sometimes found. Style is tenuous, however. It comes from within. You can't go out and acquire it. Style and fashion may share a dream, but they are created differently. Style is about an invisible promise . . .

—John Berger, *Here Is Where We Meet*

I wonder what happens to all the people who make the buttons.   —Andy Warhol

THE MASTER
OF US ALL

PROLOGUE

Cristóbal Balenciaga (1895–1972) was considered the greatest couturier of his time: in the words of Christian Dior,
"the master of us all." But the man himself remains mysterious, though private is perhaps the word he would have
preferred. "Do not waste yourself in society," he told his
friend the fabric designer Gustav Zumsteg, and followed
his own advice. Two of the things about him that one can
state with absolute certainty are that he had sinus trouble
and that he loved to ski.

Some said he was tall, others short; he was either portly
or gaunt, charming or aloof. Although he sat for Cartier-
Bresson and Man Ray he fled photographers, and some journalists claimed that he paid the newspaper vendor across
from his apartment to wave a feather duster if any were
lurking in the street below. He never took a bow at the end
of a collection, and so few people had even seen him. He
was, says *Women's Wear Daily*'s retired publisher John B.
Fairchild, a strange duck.

It got to the point where some fashion writers wondered
if he was a real person, while others thought that, like
Shakespeare, he was several. In fifty years as a designer he

never gave an interview. There must have been some explanation for the incalculable beauty of his clothes, but of course none could be found. And none would have been sought had he remained in his native Spain, esteemed but forgotten by now. Instead, he came to Paris, and Paris had, for nearly three hundred years, been the fashion capital of the world.

I daresay Italy was as qualified in terms of invention and taste, but it was not unified under a single leader. France's ascendancy began when Louis XIV's finance minister, Jean-Baptiste Colbert, informed the king that the silk weavers of Lyons were as valuable to the French economy as the gold mines of Peru were to Spain. Inventing endless and costly rules for court dress, the king easily made fashion a national preoccupation. By the mid-nineteenth century, because the silk makers had threatened to strike, Napoléon III insisted that the Empress Eugénie wear Charles Frederick Worth's enormously wide silk skirts. The empress referred to them as her *toilettes politiques.*

Having shown that it had a use, fashion came to have a meaning. It spoke volumes to Balzac and Baudelaire and Proust. The symbolist poet Stéphane Mallarmé founded a fashion magazine and provided all its contents under such pseudonyms as Marguerite de Ponty and Miss Satin. Leading French philosophers of the latter twentieth century wrote about fashion, most notably the semiologist Roland Barthes, whose article on Chanel versus Courrèges is said to have boosted the younger designer's sales: "The unchanging 'chic' of Chanel tells us that the woman has already lived (and has known how to); the obstinate 'brand-newness' of Courrèges that she is going to live," he explained.

According to Chanel, Paul Valéry had decreed that a woman wearing the wrong perfume has no future, and even at a lower level fashion made its point: in 1936 a policeman refused to arrest a feminist who chained herself to a railing at the Longchamp races. "I couldn't arrest her," he stated. "She was dressed by Molyneux."

1936: this was the year that Balenciaga moved to Paris and found an alert and avid clientele, expert seamstresses, and superb *fournisseurs* (it has been estimated that he regularly used fifty-five fabric manufacturers, twelve embroiderers, and six makers of such trimmings as feathers, fringes, and lace). Fashion was an integral part of French cultural display, and Paris was the fashion theater of the world. Balenciaga moved quickly to center stage. "If a woman came in in a Balenciaga dress, no other woman in the room existed," Diana Vreeland wrote.

He didn't follow the scene because he *was* the scene. He demanded that his designs, not himself, get the attention, which led to misunderstandings and a good deal of myth making from fashion editors in need of copy and from clients he refused to meet. If fashion is rooted in change and is deliberately delusional, his work was like a steady beacon even when it was—and it could be—downright bizarre. By 1962, American *Vogue* gave up trying to define his art and simply titled a four-page spread in its April issue "The Balenciaga Mystique":

Whatever it takes to hold vast numbers of women in the palm of your hand year after year, Balenciaga has it—to a degree that politicans and matinée idols might study with profit. Not that his clothes are easy to wear; on the contrary, they could hardly be more demanding—of elegance, wit, real clothes authority. Nor do they bristle with news; the changes he makes each season are usually just significant enough to make it dazzlingly clear that a woman in a this-year Balenciaga is a woman in touch with some of the soundest—and, possibly, most prophetic—fashion thinking of her time.

Balenciaga was an upright man of humble background, slight education, innate dignity, and a very thin skin. He never realized how useful a mask can be: when his close friend Hubert de Givenchy gave him a Picasso drawing and asked if he would like to meet the painter, Balenciaga recoiled: "He is always wearing disguises," he said. "The man is a clown."

A deeply observant Catholic (he even made a shroud for a statue of Saint Roseline in Provence), he had a feeling for ritual and for the large gesture. He despised useless detail; he spoke little. From this there grew a public image of finicky austerity and frequent descriptions of his fashion house as a monastery or church. Exaggerated, and yet his clothes had what only can be called a mystical, even a moral, effect on some of his high-stepping clients. Diana Vreeland found biblical implications in the harmony of his clothes: "women are suddenly feeling perfectly at one with creation." Mrs. Paul ("Bunny") Mellon said his dresses gave her courage, Gloria Guinness wondered whether she was good enough to wear them, and Claudia Heard de Osborne in Texas declared that she wanted to be buried in a favorite Balenciaga so that she would be properly dressed when she met Cristóbal in heaven. Pauline de Rothschild, who was dressed by Balenciaga for twenty-three years, said, "I knew and loved other dressmakers and understood them, but the mysteries were Balenciaga's."

His friends and employees emphasize his allure. He was also very trying: a collaborator remembers Balenciaga in a London restaurant sending back the sole three times. His demands were harsh but—such is the way of genius—he was hardest on himself, seeking an invisible, and possibly unattainable, goal. His staff often suffered and were always devoted, even when they had to submit to searches to make sure they weren't leaving work with secret patterns or designs.

His technique was inimitable. Only a few years ago in London, a seamstress working on a dress for a Balenciaga exhibition noticed that the apparently straight seam of a narrow dress was, when examined from the inside, intricately curved to suit the client's less than slim body.

So what to make of him when the words of fashion experts (I am not one) so often failed and when so little evidence of his private life remains? There is today, it is true, the acclaimed ready-to-wear house called Balenciaga in his old premises on the Avenue George V, but he knew that the glory of haute couture ended with him and he expressed, vainly, the wish that his name die, too. There are elegiac Balenciaga exhibitions and even a Balenciaga museum in his birthplace. And yet where is Balenciaga? Where, outside the secrecy of his studio, can we ever find the man?

We can't, and it would be disrespectful to try. But rather than examine his twice-yearly collections, we can try to see him in his times and among his staff and suppliers, "the people who make the buttons." The aim is not to explain the inexplicable but to celebrate it. Those who admire him want to know·him better, aware that we cannot really know him at all. A paradox, and mighty unsatisfactory, but also a homage of sorts—to the art, the discretion, and even the contradictions of the man.

The idea of trying to sketch Balenciaga within the historical events of his time (which he, typically, tried to ignore) and in the context of his house came during many luncheons with Florette Chelot, his top vendeuse, or saleswoman, and the first person he hired in Paris. When we began taping her memories she was in her nineties, with an amazingly clear recall of her thirty-one years with Balenciaga and sharp, though generous, judgment. As she told me in detail about the little realities of daily life at the Avenue George V and the interplay between designer and client and staff—no one before had thought to ask her—suddenly what I had noticed or read about the house of Balenciaga fell into a different perspective, and it became a living place rather than a church.

So this is also very much a double portrait: the search for Balenciaga and the story of Florette, whom I had met when I was a job-hunting New Yorker just out of college, introduced by a young Englishman about town who took me over to the Avenue George V to meet her. She was so kind, so amused by my shyness (and probably also so dismayed by my styleless dress) that she promptly went to the leftovers box and fished out a suit for me at a bargain-basement price.

This continued for a few years, until Balenciaga closed in 1968. I suppose that by then I owned about a dozen Balenciagas, most of them ending up in thrift shops because museums weren't interested in Balenciaga's plainer dresses and I had no place to keep them over eleven Paris apartment changes. Although I had no clothes left, I did happen on a snapshot of me in a beautiful collarless gray and white tweed coat. My memory was that it looked terrific, but the picture showed that I had ruined the clean neckline by leaving it open and hanging down like an extra flap of skin. My dress collar peeped out, headed toward my left ear.

I found the photo irresistibly comic and brought it to Florette for a laugh. Suddenly she was talking in her soothing old vendeuse voice: *"Mais non,"* she said, "what a charming idea to invent that lapel." Some time later, I was foolish enough to mention the picture again, and in her normal voice she sighed. "Monsieur Balenciaga would have torn that coat off your back," she said.

I

Cristóbal Balenciaga: a beautiful name. *Elle* magazine rhapsodized in 1950 that the four syllables of "Balenciaga" simply burst forth upon the page (actually, there are five), while a contemporary poet sees in the name's "swaying melody the flowing quality of Balenciaga's clothes and exquisite *justesse* of their proportions." It is a once-upon-a-time sort of name that should be part of a fable, and it is.

The setting is the humble fishing village of Getaria on Spain's Basque coast, between San Sebastián and Bilbao, the date early in the last century. The fairy tale has many versions, but let Pauline de Rothschild, the former Pauline Potter, begin:

In the center of a street made dark by the shadows of its thick stone houses, a woman was walking, her back turned to the light from the sea. She wore a pale, ankle length, silk shantung suit. The severe houses enclosed her, shuttered.

A boy was watching her.

She would come almost abreast of him, and he would run up a side-street of the fishing village, so closely carved into the mountain that its streets are as steep and narrow as Genoa's, some entirely made of steps. Down another he would run and be ahead of her again.

Then he would stare.

One day he stopped her, and asked if he could make a suit for her. The boy was about thirteen, with dark hair and darker eyes and the smile he would keep all his life.

"Why do you want to do this?" she asked.

"Because I think I can," he answered.

The boy was Cristóbal Balenciaga . . .

The woman was the old Marquesa de Casa Torres (or her daughter-in-law) and she was wearing a white (or beige) Worth, Drecoll, Ceruit, or Redfern dress or suit, according to who is telling the tale. She was possibly on her way to (or from) Mass. The boy may have been as young as six (or as old as nineteen), and his father—who had died of a heart attack or was drowned at sea—was either a fisherman or the captain of the royal yacht. Cheeky young Cristóbal, the legend continues, copied her outfit so perfectly that the marquesa became his patron and took him while he was still in his teens to meet the great couturier Jacques Doucet in Paris.

Some of this is true.

But much of it isn't. The very plainness of plain fact has never seemed to fit someone so exotic as Balenciaga (as if the amazing could not spring from the quotidian), and so for decades the legends were embellished rather than investigated. Then a young Basque curator named Miren

Arzalluz took the trouble to dig into official records and in 2010 published her findings about Balenciaga's family and early years. Myths, uncovered facts, and one's own instinct about the mix can finally make a coherent, if spare, whole.

Getaria, Balenciaga's birthplace, is a modest and handsome fishing village whose past as a whaling port brought it sufficient wealth to have as its center an oversize Gothic church, San Salvador, of surpassing gloom and considerable weirdness because its near-trapezoidal floor tilts noticeably up toward the altar. A statue near the city hall honors the local hero, Sebastián de Elcano, the first captain to circumnavigate the globe (as Magellan's second in command he took over when Magellan was killed in the Philippines), and new plaques mark the birthplaces of Balenciaga, in a tidy small house near the church, and the mother of Plácido Domingo, over an anchovy cannery. Getaria has excellent fish that restaurateurs grill in the street, and gray buildings whose sound proportions and straightness of line are bolder than the often-quaint Basque architecture of France. Even now Getaria has an air of provincial rectitude; its inhabitants provided San Sebastián, thirty kilometers along the coast, with fish and services when the Spanish king and his court went there each summer.

In about 1853, France's Empress Eugénie, who was born in Spain, invented Biarritz as a fashionable resort. Following her example, in 1887, Queen María Cristina of Spain decided to make San Sebastián, across the border, the official summer home of the Spanish court. While Biarritz is dramatic and citified, San Sebastián is calmer and more elegant, with a wide seafront and restaurants that have made it a foodie mecca today. Friends in Paris were often surprised by the supposedly austere Balenciaga's pleasure in good eating, but he was Basque, and three existential questions, it is said, trouble the Basques each day: Where do we come from? Who are we? What are we going to have for dinner?

The last question results in excellent local cooking; the first two are harder. No one knows where the Basques come from—even the prevalent blood type differs from that of other Europeans—and they like to think of themselves as Europe's aborigines, their spiritual locus being an ancient oak tree in Guernica. The Basques' language, Euskera, once believed to be the tongue spoken in the Garden of Eden, bears no relation to any other, and they group all the other languages in the world in one single dismissive word,

Beachgoers at San Sebastián, circa 1900

Erdera. They are proud (by an ancient royal Spanish edict they are all aristocrats), deeply Catholic, and intractable. Cristóbal Balenciaga was definitely Basque.

The family was modest but respected: his father, a fisherman, served briefly as mayor of Getaria and rose to skipper the launch that was often used by the Spanish court, including the queen, in the summer season. His mother bore five children, two of whom died in infancy. Cristóbal, born in 1895, was the youngest; his sister, Agustina, and his brother, Juan Martín, remained his business associates in Spain throughout their lives. The older children were already at work when their father died after a stroke, leaving eleven-year-old Cristóbal alone to help out his mother, Martina Eizaguirre.

Well before her husband's death Martina was already giving sewing lessons to local girls and making dresses for private clients such as the Marquesa de Casa Torres, whose dressmaker she became a year before before Cristóbal was born. Hubert de Givenchy says that Balenciaga told him that his first attempt at design was to make a necklace for his cat ("but since you can't make a cat lie on its back all the beads scattered"), while a French magazine claims that he began by making a coat, including the legs, for his dog (presumably an early manifestation of his passion for sleeves). In any event the boy was at home with his mother, helping out, playing with scraps of fabric, and often going with her for fittings in the homes of summering aristocrats.

So the long-accepted legend of the meeting between the marquesa and the boy must be replaced by more convincing fact: he knew the marquesa and her home, just up the hill from the center of Getaria, from childhood. While he was helping his mother or playing with the marquesa's children, he took in her wardrobe and her fashion magazines and her well-chosen furnishings (the marqués owned paintings by Goya and Velásquez), plugging naturally into the world of high style where he would spend his life. Not only could he study the Paris gowns his mother copied for summer use, but he could also learn to appreciate English tailoring and take in such novelties as department stores and buying by catalog, both of which the marquesa enjoyed.

Although he was never at ease with the French *gratin*, or upper crust, from her he picked up a comfortable familiarity with the Spanish aristocracy: it was of course Balenciaga who made the wedding dress of the marquesa's great-grandaughter, Fabiola, when she married the king of the Belgians in 1960, and a few years later one of his models was astonished to see, on the salon's white sofa, the taciturn Balenciaga laughing and chatting away with an elderly lady who turned out to be Victoria Eugenia, the former queen of Spain.

Through the marquesa, the twelve-year-old Balenciaga apprenticed with a San Sebastián tailor, then moved on to a tonier shop called New England, and to the new San Sebastián branch of the Grand Magasins du Louvre department store, which was patronized not only by the marquesa but by María Cristina, the dowager queen. By 1913 he was being sent to Paris as a buyer. After a short spell in Bordeaux to learn French, in 1918 he opened his first salon, C. Balenciaga, in San Sebastián, then went into a six-year partnership with two sisters who provided most of the backing. Balenciaga's investment was 7,362 pesetas and 25 céntimos, the 25 cents recalling that if his reputation was growing, his finances were still tight. When the six-year contract ended in 1924, he was able to open a new house, Cristóbal Balenciaga, gradually creating branches in Madrid and Barcelona under his name or under variations of Eisa, a reworking of his mother's maiden name.

The timing was just right. While most of Europe agonized in World War I, Spain, which remained neutral, flourished, especially San Sebastián, enriched by the wealth of Bilbao, a port and a banking and industrial center, and by the well-heeled of all nations who came to bask in its elegance and ease. Old-timers such as the duchess, who went to Paris each year to order 365 hats (366 in leap year), would disappear after the war, but the new crowd was avid and deeply attractive to Paris couturiers who, starting in 1917, arrived with their collections. The major houses of Callot, Paquin, and Worth showed in such luxury hotels as the Maria Cristina, and Balenciaga saw, and possibly met, Chanel at San Sebastián's casino. Most important, he began a lifelong friendship with Madeleine Vionnet, the first designer to use the bias cut on the body of a dress, fashion's equivalent of inventing the wheel.

Balenciaga probably met Vionnet when she showed her collection to the Spanish court at San Sebastián in 1920. He was already buying her clothes for his shop on his Paris trips (a hasty working sketch on a piece of hotel stationery in the Arts Décoratifs archive in Paris also suggests that he was not above pinching her ideas), but when they met and she saw his work she encouraged him to create rather than adapt other people's designs. They shared a stubborn and exalted view of clothes as a sort of second skin that

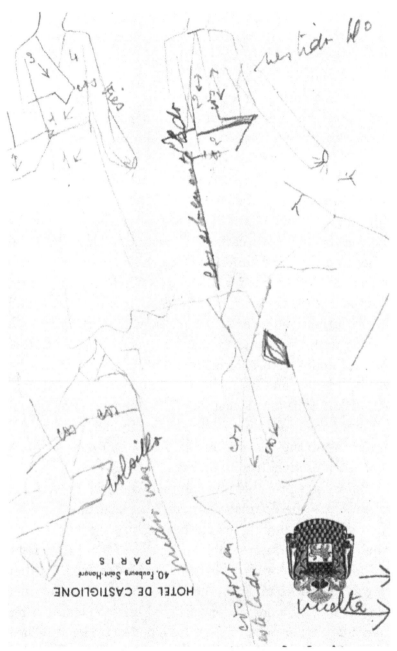

Balenciaga copies a dress on a buying trip to Paris

sculpts, rather than encases, the body: the couturier as a builder, not a decorator. They were both brilliant technicians, Balenciaga the more versatile in that he was as expert at tailoring coats and suits as at cutting soft fabrics, and both saw the designer as a craftsman dealing with clients and not as a remote artist. "A couturier dresses human beings, not dreams," Vionnet would say. Their friendship lasted until Balenciaga's death, and when I met Vionnet in the late 1960s she was just back from a two-week stay in Balenciaga's country house near Orléans to recover from bronchitis and was wearing a floor-length bias-cut wool crepe skirt and matching vest that he had made for her in bright red (her own palette tended to shades of beige).

They were of equal historical importance—if Dior later called Balenciaga "the master of us all," he also said "no one has carried the art of dressmaking farther than Vionnet"—but she was a generation older, having been born in 1876, and was already approaching glory when they met. Their clothes were dissimilar, Vionnet specializing in richly simple Greek-style folds, a deliciously errant vestal look, but they shared ardor and integrity—"a dress must be sincere," Vionnet said—and had so intense an understanding of fabrics that neither of them liked to sketch. "I hate sketching. Designers who sketch have no feeling for fabric," Vionnet said. Instead, she draped her fabrics on a wooden doll 31.5 inches tall, and Givenchy told me that when she was very old and bedridden and Balenciaga came to visit, she would show him something she had just confected on the doll with the wish that it might be useful to him. "And Cristóbal, with that marvelous smile, would say to me, Isn't it adorable that at her age this woman would continue to work and give me her models," Givenchy said. "He had until the end of his life someone who counted enormously for him, and that was Madame Vionnet."

To the young Balenciaga, Vionnet must have seemed like a favorite teacher, firm but kind, and indeed she had hoped to teach, but a neighbor pointed out to her father (her mother had run off) that further studies would mean more clothing bills, so at the age of ten she was yanked out of school and apprenticed to a dressmaker. "If I had become a professor I would just have had a brain," she said many years later. "Instead I discovered my hands and learned to love them." In England to pick up the language, she became an attendant in a lunatic asylum, then worked for five years in Kate Reilly's dressmaking establishment

Madeleine Vionnet

on Dover Street in London. Returning to Paris, she was engaged by the prestigious Callot Soeurs, then hired away by Jacques Doucet, a very grand designer and collector (he was an early patron of the furniture designer Eileen Gray and the first owner of *Les Demoiselles d'Avignon*), in order to modernize his house. It was there that she discovered that the bias cut, a version of which had been used only to line garments, could give fabrics a new fluidity: "I wanted it and found it," she told me. "It seemed natural." The vendeuses, she added, hated it. In 1912 she opened her own modest house on the Rue de Rivoli and in 1923 got backing to become the first couturier on the Avenue Montaigne.

The House of Vionnet, at number 50, towered over its neighbors and triumphed in the architectural press as a perfect example of steel and glass Art Deco. It had 1,900 employees and 43 ateliers. While the grand salon of a house like Callot was heavy and crowded with furniture, Vionnet had a vast clean space framed with arches bordered in Lalique glass. When it came to opening his Paris house, Balenciaga followed Vionnet in keeping his public rooms simple and his private studio strictly off-limits. He did not follow Vionnet's more compassionate innovations—a free staff cafeteria, medical service, and child care as well as classes for those who, like her, had had to leave school too young. Since he shared her loathing for copyists, having himself been one on a modest scale, he adopted her practice of photographing each model with its number, flat police lineup pictures, though he did not, like Vionnet, put his thumbprint on the label of every dress he made.

Vionnet was stronger and more authoritative than the

young Balenciaga—he would not have said "I have never seen a fabric that refused to obey me," even though it was true—and it was her strength and encouragement that helped him free his fantasy and develop his prodigious technique.

Discovering his talents, the young Balenciaga had great success—by the age of twenty-one he is said to have dressed the queen of Spain—and success brought a confidence he lost in his later days when his sole, and impossible, rival was his glorious self. After each new collection in the 1950s and '60s, people recalled, he would be tearful and tense because it hadn't been up to his standard. In all, it was a dog's life, he said after his retirement. But when he was young and imperfect, all he had to do was get better, and he did.

And he found love. Probably on a buying trip to Paris he met a charming and well-connected young man with sleek dark hair, Wladzio Jaworowski d'Attainville, with whom he would live for some twenty years. D'Attainville was Polish-French; his mother, according to a story in American *Vogue* in the 1940s, entertained in style and was photographed grandly under a portrait of Princess Ghika, her grandmother. Wladzio joined Balenciaga and Balenciaga's sister and brother in the Spanish company, designed witty hats, and smoothly made contacts that Balenciaga, less experienced, was still awkward about.

Early Balenciaga is not exciting (his first extant design, made in 1912 when he was seventeen, is a stiff but correct floor-length black suit with a jabot of boned lace). He was forming the rock-solid base that made his later vanguard designs so appealing and convincing. And he

Balenciaga's Paris portrait, 1927

knew intimately the needs of his well-off and conservative clientele.

By 1927, when he was important enough to have his portrait made, he did not commission a local but went to Paris and sat for Boris Lipnitzki, the fashionable celebrity photographer of Poiret, Schiaparelli, Cocteau, and Chanel. The resulting series shows a gracile, perfectly tailored, and easeful young man of great beauty, with fine hands, a long fastidious upper lip, and heavy brows crowning limpid and myopic dark eyes.

It was a golden new world, and there were cracks in it. The year that Balenciaga posed for Lipnitzki he opened a less expensive second house for a younger clientele in San Sebastián, since the dictator Miguel Primo de Rivera, ruling as prime minister with the complicity of the king, had cut into the luxury trade by closing the casino. Worse, much worse, was to come. There is no conflict more dreadful than a civil war, and in Spain the tremors began soon after the Second Republic—the last freely elected Spanish government for forty years—took over in April 1931.

The economy, mismanaged by Primo de Rivera, was deeply in trouble: the peseta had lost nearly 50 percent of its value, unemployment was rising while industrial production fell, and the Morgan bank had cancelled a $60 million loan. Francisco Franco—Europe's youngest general since Napoléon—was waiting in the wings.

Franco indicated that he would restore King Alfonso XIII, who had been best man at his wedding, and many early supporters believed that he would bring back the good old days, the sturdy status quo. Like most craftsmen in luxury trades, Balenciaga was as conservative as his patrons and—as he showed later during the Occupation of Paris—totally indifferent to politics. Franco detested the unruly Basques, displaying the gravest cruelty when he allowed his German allies to test their new aircraft by bombing Guernica and its sacred oak tree, symbol of Basque unity, on a sunny market day in April 1937. But Franco's wife, the nearly aristocratic Carmen Polo, was a Balenciaga client from as early as 1933, when he made her a long bias-cut black faille gown for the ceremony at which her husband took command of the Balearic Islands. The last dress he ever made, weeks before his death in 1972, was her granddaughter's wedding gown.

The houses of Balenciaga—he had opened branches in Madrid and Barcelona while continuing to live in San Sebastián—remained open during the sieges of both cities. In San Sebastián, which Franco bombed by air and sea, there was deadly street fighting and the stench of war invaded even the Maria Cristina hotel, scene of so many fashion shows, where it was claimed that Franquists used live bodies as sandbags. By mid-September 1936, refugees were fleeing by the thousands and Balenciaga was among them, surely not for political reasons but because he knew that luxury trades do not flourish during a civil war.

He decided to head for Paris with Nicolás and Virgilia Bizcarrondo, whom *Vogue*'s Bettina Ballard says he met in a bomb shelter but who were in fact neighbors in his apartment building. Nicolás, a militant Republican opposed to Franco, was a balding engineer with a knobby, pleasant face; his wife was comfortably plump and wealthy and had a sister living in Paris. Wladzio had his excellent social connections. So why not relocate?

The Bizcarrondos in the 1950s

The usual view is that the Balenciaga who left Spain in 1936 was a gifted tyro who bloomed in the creative air of Paris, but in truth he was already a seasoned success, forty-one years old. Legend also portrays him as a dreamy recluse remote from money matters, but he had proved his business skills by creating—and, when necessary, discarding—no fewer than seven houses during his Spanish years, shrewdly adapting from couture to semi-ready-to-wear as the times demanded. And anyway there was never a question of shutting down Balenciaga/Spain, or a doubt that he would return when the unpleasantness was over.

The Paris they found was nominally peaceful but so bestirred by economic and political problems that the word revolution was muttered, if not said aloud. The scandal caused by the financial outrages of the Stavisky affair in 1934 had revealed widescale corruption and was followed by a general strike, violent anti-Semitism, riots in the Place de la Concorde—the worst since the Commune of 1871—and the selection as prime minister a few months before Balenciaga arrived of Léon Blum, a man whose probity and humanity ensured that his tenure would be brief. Even the house of Chanel went on strike, its workers demanding that Mademoiselle receive their delegates. She refused on the grounds that the word delegate was unfamiliar to her. It was a tired, rotting world mad for something new. "It was this that made the thirties so memorable," Janet Flanner wrote, "for what was new automatically became a fresh formula for new memories." A good moment for a fresh face on the fashion scene.

Balenciaga found space on the third floor of 10 Avenue George V, a few blocks from Vionnet and next to Mainbocher, whose quarters he would take over after World War II. The first person he hired was a twenty-five-year-old vendeuse with brown hair, a competent air set off by a smile at once delighted and comforting, and a black order book from her previous job at her mother-in-law's fashion house. Her name was Florette Chelot.

"I was recommended by a friend in the fabric business," Florette told me. "I arrive, I find a very handsome and charming man who speaks French rather badly. He is in a big bare space which later became two workrooms, seated on a stool in front of a trestle table filled with swatches of fabric. He said, I am sorry I cannot offer you a chair

10 Avenue George V

because this stool and table is all there is. He didn't even have any ateliers then.

"So we chatted and got to know each other. I told him about myself, that I knew the métier from my mother-in-law and I knew the business side from working with sales offices." Her black book included such names as Mme César Ritz, Bloomingdales, and Harrods. "He immediately said fine and I said, If you agree, I'll start making contacts with clients and buyers." He agreed and offered her a 10 percent commission on sales.

"When he saw what I sold after the first collection he cut me down to five percent because he said otherwise I'd be earning more than he did." In later years Balenciaga's bookkeeper would tell Florette that her sales accounted for half the earnings of the couture house.

Florette was born Amélie Flore Delion in Burgundy, in the village of Égriselles-le-Bocage, where her mother ran a small hotel for commercial travelers and Florette went to the local school in her black sateen smock buttoned in the back and wooden shoes. "I loved my sabots, I used to admire my feet as I walked and decorate them with flowers. In the winter I used them as skis." When the weather was fine the neighbors would sit outdoors and Florette would go from house to house and sing to them.

It was a sunny and loving childhood. Then her mother died in 1918 from Spanish flu: "I was happy until the age of seven" is how Florette put it. Her grieving father sold the hotel, bought another, and then died when she was eleven, leaving her in the charge of her older sister. She left school unwillingly and at fifteen was in Paris living in a pension her sister found on the Rue Eugène Carrière in Montmartre, where the girls had to cover their bodies in a gown when they took a bath and dinner was vegetable soup with no vegetables. She quickly found work as a telephonist at the new Paris buying office of the New York merchant Henri Bendel, although she had nothing much to recommend her aside from doggedness, a good nature, and tidy handwriting of which she remained proud all her life.

The very first day at work a charming older man of twenty-four named Pierre Chelot showed her how to plug the wires into the switchboard and how to address telephone operators. He became her Pygmalion and, in 1931, her husband, but at first he was simply her mentor. Pierre, nicknamed Payot, was the son of a top fitter at Callot Soeurs, where his father was a director, and had always worked on the edge of fashion. Employed by a silk maker in Lyons, he

The salon, or showroom, at Balenciaga

was charged with introducing a local seamstress, Yvette Labrousse, the recently crowned Miss France, to the Paris couture. She later married the Aga Khan and became one of Florette's best clients.

Florette took night classes at Berlitz and in 1929 went briefly to England, where she improved her English by learning popular songs. "I cahnt geeve you enyseeng baht loove, babby," she sang to me in her chirpy voice over lunch in a bistro near her flat on the Île St. Louis while telling about her stay in Sussex. Sometimes, she once said, she wished she had been an actress, and I could imagine her not as a leading lady but as the soubrette in an operetta, saucy and warmhearted. There was indeed a touch of theater in her Balenciaga days when, in shining her full at-

The salon at Callot Soeurs

tention on the client, she in turn became the focus for that client, as if she were onstage. She liked it and did it spectacularly well.

Payot saw to her education, even getting her to read Proust, and introduced her to his mother, who renamed her Florette and whom she adored. "You who have a family cannot imagine what it was like for me to find one," she told me. Henriette Chelot, a fine-looking woman in her Callot dresses and Hellstern shoes, might have hoped that her only son would make a more advantageous match, but even when Florette fell ill with tuberculosis of the uterus and became unable to bear children, Mme Chelot encouraged the marriage, gave the young couple a big engagement reception at the Hotel George V, and took them into

Florette on the scene

her home at St. Cloud. And it was thanks to her that Florette became a vendeuse in the haute couture.

The old house of Callot Soeurs, with its crowded showroom in which furniture and rugs were on sale as well as clothes, was fading, so Mme Chelot and a friend opened their own small house, Marie-Henriette, off the Place Vendôme with a modern salon, Coromandel screens like Chanel's, and a good clientele from Callot. There was one fatal problem: it was 1936 and the rioting in the nearby Place de la Concorde was scaring off foreign clients and buyers. Marie-Henriette closed and Florette went to see Balenciaga at the Avenue George V.

When Balenciaga opened, there were three vendeuses: Florette; the much older Marthe, who had dressed the relentlessly stylish Mrs. Harrison Williams at Paquin; and Maria. In couture tradition, each house had a vendeuse who had fallen on hard times and was invited everywhere because she had had *malheurs* and knew everyone. Maria was Balenciaga's *grande dame qui a eu des malheurs*, a Spanish friend of his who had had an unhappy affair with a toreador. She wasn't much at selling but she got around. Since they worked on commission the vendeuses were rivals. Florette was a very nice woman, but she could be tough when necessary, which was all too often.

By house custom the vendeuses were given two black work dresses a year from the previous collection, but they had to pay for the fabric. Their job was to sell, obviously, but it was a job that required a certain complicity with the client, which some carried to a form of mimesis or even—odd in view of the clients' wealth and frequent bad manners—pity. Much later, the flinty-eyed Odette, for example, would remark on how sorry she felt for Liz Taylor, all dressed up and tearful as she waited in their hotel suite for Richard Burton to down another last drink. Florette had a favorite client, the Baroness Alain de Rothschild, but she served all comers equally. During our talks she never said "I sold a client a dress," but instead "I made her a dress" or "I dressed her."

"Just selling isn't interesting, it sounds like a grocery store. A good vendeuse knows how to win the confidence and fidelity of her client. We were part of their lives, we often knew their husbands, their children, their best friends. They knew we wanted them to be at their best." If they weren't, Balenciaga blamed the vendeuse.

The directrice, of the new house, brought in by

d'Attainville, was the pretty Baroness d'Echtall, who was replaced after World War II by the redoubtable Mlle Renée Tamisier with her firm ways and granitic smile. It was Renée who ran the day-to-day operations, translating Balenciaga's need for privacy into a house policy of paranoia. There were three ateliers: in tailoring, Denis, who remained until 1954, and in soft fabrics, Claude and Suzanne, who were there until the end. (Employees tended to stay as long with Balenciaga as they could.)

Balenciaga always chose his house models himself, the first and favorite being the alarming Colette, who only stopped modeling in 1954: bony and long-waisted (unusual for a French woman of that time), she would crash into the showroom like an invading army. Her jutting pelvic bones inspired Balenciaga's early use of padded hips, while her long neck and curved spine were the origin of his famous set-back neckline and bloused back, which, with a semi-fitted front, was to be a boon to so many aging women over the coming years. (As Gloria Guinness later pointed out, the framelike neckline allowed women and their pearls to breathe, while the shortened sleeve uncovered their bracelets and the unemphatic waistline permitted them to "believe in a figure that perhaps they did not have").

Like Vionnet, Balenciaga wanted his models to be remote rather than appealing, gazing over the heads of clients and casually carrying a card on which the number of the outfit—unlike other designers, he never gave his clothes names—was displayed. He invented a signature loping walk for them, long strides, torso tilted back, pelvis thrust forward. "They walk with a pleasant swagger—the likable swagger of the aristocrat," *Women's Journal* commented

Colette, Balenciaga's favorite model

I recognized the walk at once when I was strolling one day with the former Renée Bousquet, then nearly eighty. She was Basque and still a teenager when she left Grès, where she was not happy, for Balenciaga, where she was. In those early days it was an easygoing and happy place. "It was a family," she said. "The Bizcarrondos were *des gens parfaits*, d'Attainville was adorable and animated the place, Balenciaga was very discreet and never forward in any way. He knew how to do everything, and he did." His sense of humor in those times was a bit rough. When young Renée complained to him about a photographer's wandering hands he simply burst out laughing, and when she told him she was leaving to marry a businessman, Henri Le Roux, instead of offering good wishes he told her she could come back if it didn't work out. She did come back, some years later, but just to have Balenciaga meet her children.

M. Bizcarrondo took care of the house's finances; his wife was a discreet and useful presence who helped Balenciaga smooth off his rough edges and who, after the success of the first collection, wrapped and delivered the orders with Florette. Although older than the Chelots, the Bizcarrondos often went boating with them (the Chelots were enthusiastic canoers—Payot even ordered a canoe from Canada—preferring the early spring when business was slow and the rivers of central France ran high). The Bizcarrondos, people said, were the heart of the house.

The Chelots were even friendly with Balenciaga. "In those days he was charming, we were a team," Florette said. They dined often at Ramponneau, across the street from where Balenciaga and d'Attainville lived at 28 Avenue Marceau (the Bizcarrondos lived at number 26). "He

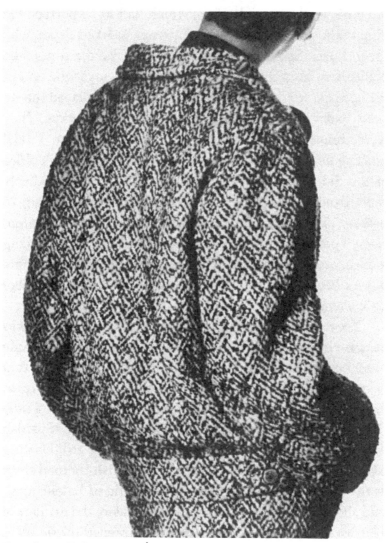

The classic Balenciaga suit jacket

liked his food, especially fish, which had to be perfect. He didn't talk of much besides couture but he liked Payot, who spoke fluent Spanish, and I was quiet." Before dinner he made them his dry martinis. "It was Balenciaga who taught me how. He would take a napkin on which he placed the ice cubes to dry them off so that there was no excess water. They were almost pure gin. Payot didn't much like them. I did."

The new house had been registered at the clerk's office of the Seine commercial court on July 7, 1937, modestly capitalized at 100,000 francs with Bizcarrondo holding 75 percent of the shares, d'Attainville 20 percent, and Balenciaga 5 percent. Its first collection was shown the following month, attended mostly by the press and department store buyers because private clients had no idea who Cristóbal Balenciaga was.

They soon found out who he was, but *what* he was became increasingly harder to define as his work became more original and unclassifiable. The default term is that he was very Spanish. Jessica Daves, the editor of *Vogue*, referred vaguely but authoritatively in a *New York Times* story on the closing of his house in 1968 to his "Spanish way of thinking." Diana Vreeland, writing to "Darling Mona" (Bismarck) in 1973 about her Spanish-themed show at the Metropolitan Museum, "The World of Balenciaga," said she had "Goyas, Valesquez [sic], Picasso, the armour of Charles I on a huge white horse—Flamenco music plays faintly and one hears heels and castanets clicking . . ." Marie-Andrée Jouve, in her 1989 book, detailed the influence of Goya and Velásquez and Zurbarán; Oscar de la Renta, who had worked briefly as a sketch artist for Balenciaga in Madrid, said that his work "remained to the core very Spanish." De la Renta was talking about the exhibition of which he was honorary president, "Balenciaga: Spanish Master," shown in New York and San Francisco in 2010–2011. The show's curator and Balenciaga expert, Hamish Bowles, omitted the castanets but showed dresses before a photomontage of Getaria and made juxtapositions with Spanish painters, including the abstract shapes of a Miró with the famous four-sided envelope dress of 1967.

"To do a show based on the influence of Spain on Balenciaga is an idea like any other—one has to find a title," Givenchy said of the exhibition. Of course Balenciaga was Spanish just as Dior was French and, for that matter, Ralph Lauren is American, but sometimes the Spanish label seems to be just that: a reductive way of positioning a talent too original for classification. He was Spanish, but above all he was Balenciaga.

Beginning with his "Infanta" dress in 1939 he did indeed call on obvious Spanish references from the bullring, from regional costume, from famous paintings. But he hated bullfights and didn't seem to have gone to the Prado except for one recorded visit, preferring flea markets where his excellent eye trumped the lack of education that made museums so trying. The Infanta dress, it can be argued, was a way of helping the press to define a newcomer, and if over the years he showed clothes based on a bullfighter's hat or a flamenco dress, it was rare. As Pamela Golbin, who curated the 2006 Balenciaga retrospective at the Musée des Arts Décoratifs in Paris, puts it, "He did do boleros, but in each show there were 150 or 200 pieces and if there were three or four boleros that didn't mean it was all straight from Spain."

The "Infanta" dress, 1939

Still, like all couturiers, Balenciaga needed the occasional showpiece as a talking point, and it was often based on a Spanish idea. "Don't order that, it's just for show," he would sometimes tell his dear Spanish friend the Marquesa de Llanzol, and he may have been talking about the bullfighter's jacket that he showed in 1946, which she ordered anyway. It was indeed a showstopper and a clever choice for that year, when the short jacket responded to postwar fabric restrictions, and its heavy embroidery was what he had been doing a great deal of under the sumptuary laws the German Occupation had imposed. It was surely intended as an attention-getting exception, not a trend.

Balenciaga's own private collection of fashion books and fabrics ranged widely over eighteenth- and nineteenth-century Europe. Since most of the antique costumes he owned had been picked up in Spanish flea markets, they are weighted toward Andalusian, Basque, and other regional designs, but he also found a fine black jacket made by a Philadelphia store called Homer LeBoutillier in around 1890, bright blue French breeches, or culottes, from 1785, a priest's maniple, a piece from a richly decorated horse's harness, and a pair of dainty embroidered mules.

Among other influences that have been discerned: Japanese woodcuts, paintings by the Impressionists, Bronzino and Lorenzo Lotto, and even George Cukor's 1934 film adaptation of Louisa May Alcott. "I found the clothes very pretty, particularly a group of long-sleeved, tight-bodiced at-home dresses that reminded me of 'Little Women,'" Bettina Ballard wrote of the first collection.

That show, relatively conventional and budget-conscious, introduced Paris to Balenciaga's fine technique and impeccable taste. "The young Spanish couturier Balenciago [*sic*] produced a notable first collection," said *Women's Wear Daily*, while the *New York Herald Tribune* detected a Goya note and *L'Officiel de la Haute Couture* thought it rather Grecian. "Knowing journalists were already saying that this quiet Spaniard was bringing a stability and elegance to a disordered fashion scene," the English journalist Madge Garland recalled much later.

The buyers bought, the magazines took pictures, Florette and Mme Bizcarrondo worked late to wrap and make deliveries, helped by a seamstress. It was a quiet triumph of just the right sort for someone who knew better than to try to rock the French fashion scene. "The first collection had nothing eccentric, it was sober and very well done," Florette said. "But," she added, "I found it a little bit dull."

2

After his first Paris collection, Balenciaga said to Florette, "We must have an *alternativa*"—a bullfighting term, she told me, that meant the second show would have to be even better. Actually, an *alternativa* is the celebratory ceremony whereby a novice bullfighter becomes a full-fledged toreador: Balenciaga knew he had arrived. For the second collection, American *Vogue* hailed his "magnificent evening gowns" while *Harper's Bazaar*, in a two-page spread, claimed "you could go down to posterity in any of these four Balenciaga dresses," even though he used too much black for American skin tones. Florette added the Duchess of Westminster to her client list, and Gloria Rubio (who with her fourth marriage to the British banker became Mrs. Loel Guinness) was soon one of the house's most durable big spenders. On Saint Catherine's Day, the traditional couture fête for employees who are still unmarried at twenty-five, Balenciaga himself was feeling so fine that he not only attended the party but swept Florette into a showy paso doble. He danced very well, she said.

The year, unfortunately, was 1938 and nothing was right in the world, which only increased the need to make

Printed rayon dress, 1938

it seem as if something were. The attempt was fevered, overdone. The newest diet? Remain in bed and eat nothing but eight to ten oranges per day. The faces *en vue?* Daisy Fellowes, the Duchess of Windsor—hard-jawed, angular, and sleek with none of the hoydenish charm of earlier years.

The great Paris World's Fair of 1937, which opened, unfinished, a month late, closed with a deficit of 200 million francs, and in 1938 Prime Minister Léon Blum was axed. The fair, he had declared, would deal a death blow to fascism. It included massive Nazi and Soviet pavilions, a salute to the haute couture, which had ten thousand workers out of jobs, Fred Astaire and Ginger Rogers dropping by to dance away all angst, and, in the Spanish pavilion, Picasso's *Guernica.* For the writer Michel Leiris, Picasso was sending a warning: "Everything we love is about to die."

In its sidelong way, fashion can be eerily predictive—after all, it's about what will be and not about what is—and perhaps someone should have felt a warning earlier in the decade when Bavarian dress was the mode while Hitler's power grew. English gentlemen wore lederhosen and women dirndls until *Harper's Bazaar* sternly disavowed them—"we loved the dirndl well, but not too wisely"—after Austria was invaded. The cunningly daft inventions of Schiaparelli, a longtime antifascist, may have been a warning against the true lunacy to come, and even the early success of Balenciaga could owe something to a nervous wish for something fresh and new. Looking back, Madge Garland saw the fashions of the late 1930s as "absolutely frantic to explore every possibility and express every idea before it was too late. Was the play nearly over? Would the curtain come down soon?"

Very soon. There was a brief rush to being serious. In an article called "Why I Am Gorged with Glamour Photography," Cecil Beaton declared in 1938 that "I want to make photographs of very elegant women taking the grit out of their eyes, or blowing their noses, or taking the lipstick off their teeth." He didn't, of course, and, whether on the edge of the volcano or not, the dance went on. "The spring season of 1939 was the gayest I had ever seen," wrote Bettina Ballard. "There were garden parties or big cocktail parties every day and balls or some sort of spectacle every night for all of June and into July." The loveliest was given by *Harper's Bazaar*'s Louise Macy (always called Louie and later the wife of President Roosevelt's adviser Harry Hopkins) with Prince Jean-Louis de Faucigny-Lucinge as cohost. Macy, long on charm and short of cash (she had only $400 to spend), cajoled the French government into the loan for one night of a magnificent ruin, the seventeenth-century Hôtel Salé (now the Picasso museum) in the Marais, and got her friend André Terrail, owner of La Tour d'Argent, to donate food and wines. There were candlelit chandeliers and powdered footmen; guests wore tiaras, decorations, white tie and tails. Until six o'clock the following morning, the crumbling shell was a palace of dreams.

And then, soon after, on September 3, France and England declared war on Germany after the invasion of Poland and the hallucinatory period known as the Phony War began. "Gentlemen," said the French diplomat and author Paul Claudel, "in the little moment that remains to us between the crisis and catastrophe, we may as well take a glass of champagne."

Winter 1939, photographed by George Hoyningen-Huene

Catastrophe came eight months later when the Germans invaded the Netherlands, Belgium, Luxembourg, and, inevitably, France, although Maurice Privat's annual forecast had predicted that there would be no war and that 1940 would be the Year of French Grandeur. Privat, a stubby little man in droopy mouse-gray socks, had a wide following and was the private astrologer of the future prime minister Pierre Laval.

Paris fell into a tense mix of boredom and fear, and even the simplest words had no meaning. What sort of war might there be, Simone de Beauvoir asked her diary, and what does this word war really mean? There were no buses, and taxis had been commandeered to take troops, some in World War I uniform, to their posts. Nighttime was eerie, with car headlights, streetlamps, and blackout curtains colored blue to ward off aerial attack. Emerging from bomb shelters after an alert, Parisians could see their city's placid wide sky and its lovely monuments unscathed: perhaps it was all just a bad joke, a gimcrack tinsel fake of a war? The gaiety may have been nervous, but at least Paris was still gay. Until it wasn't.

Delightful luncheon parties replaced balls, and Daisy Fellowes displayed timely chic by appearing in a stunningly severe black suit. To save material the famous milliner Suzy made snoods instead of big hats. For fear of foreign spies, only French could be spoken over the telephone, and crossword puzzles were banned lest they contain coded messages. The wealthier quarters of Paris emptied as people fled south—for once it was harder to get first- than third-class train tickets—and from New York, *Vogue*'s editor, Edna Woolman Chase, cabled Bettina Ballard, "Send story

Marie-Louise Bousquet

on what smart women are wearing in air raid shelters."
Piguet was making jersey jumpsuits, Hermès offered
leather gas mask covers as well as cashmere sleeping bags,
Schiaparelli built muffs into the pockets of her dresses for
standing in icy queues, and the best bomb shelter was at
the Ritz with its fur-lined blankets. In the couturiers' sa-
lons the collections went on as usual, attended for the first
time by the dowdy wife of France's military leader, General Gamelin. As a morale booster she was a flop, since
she knitted through every show from a skein of khaki
wool.

Carmel Snow from *Harper's Bazaar* came over in January for the summer 1940 collections in order, she said, to
give the French fashion industry a boost. Her aide was the
wizened, clever Marie-Louise Bousquet, an earlier attempt
by Snow to employ Daisy Fellowes having faded when the

fabulously rich Mrs. Fellowes received buyers, if at all, reclining on her Neuilly chaise longue and wearing Chinese pajamas in peacock blue silk. (Marie-Louise Bousquet was neither rich nor elegant but she was a major mover in artistic and literary circles and a gifted gossip of the sort who doesn't embellish the truth but invents it.)

Balenciaga opened the collections, a star by now with press and buyers fighting to get in, according to London's *Daily Express. L'Officiel de la Haute Couture* praised his profound originality, and *Vogue* and *Harper's* reported purchases by Marshall Field in Chicago and Hattie Carnegie in New York, proof that he was definitely in the buyers' books. Florette's sales soared for the month of January, then slowly dropped so that in June, when the Germans marched into Paris, they were very slight, and in July and August there were none at all. Balenciaga was in Madrid attending to his Spanish houses, which remained open during the war, while Florette and the directrice stayed on to protect Avenue George V because the Germans intended to shut it down. But the Spanish embassy intervened, and because Germany was courting neutral Spain to enter the war on its side, Balenciaga was allowed to return to a Paris that was deserted and without hope. The month the Germans arrived, Florette had snapped a photo (the only one ever taken) of the three founders, Balenciaga, Bizcarrondo, and d'Attainville, smiling on the balcony at 10 Avenue George V.

The Germans had marched into Paris on June 14, 1940. It had all happened so quickly, just a month after their breakthrough at Sedan, yet the civilians at the Louvre, who had shipped their treasures to safety as early as 1938, had foreseen the debacle. A corrupt and confused government

Florette snaps the three founders in 1940: (from left to right)
Bizcarrondo, d'Attainville, and Balenciaga

and hopeless military leadership made it easy. French troops were neither outnumbered nor ill-armed: the problem was their generals, fusty relics from World War I with kepis deep in gold braid and outmoded ideas. General Gamelin, hero of the Battle of the Marne and known to his troops as Gaga-melin, refused to disturb his sleep by installing a radio or telegraph in his fortress outside Paris, and Marshal Pétain attributed the defeat to the fact that new-fangled communications had taken the place of reliable carrier pigeons.

But Pétain, the eighty-four-year-old Victor of Verdun, blue-eyed with a snowy cowcatcher mustache, occupied no military post during the defeat and so nothing was held against him, neither his views on carrier pigeons (if they were known) nor the fact that he had been the first government minister to flee Paris. Parliament voted him full powers, 569 for, 80 against, and 20 abstentions. He was the would-be restorer of an ancient moral order that had unraveled in the dislocated present and he promised redemption for past weaknesses. Short months later he was photographed shaking hands with Hitler. For many it was the sensible way. "What is the worst thing that can happen if Germany invades?" the writer Jean Giono had asked. "Become German? I'd rather be a living German than a dead Frenchman."

The good part was that the French didn't even have to become German. Under the new regime, the collaboration government, with headquarters in the spa town of Vichy, was French-run and the French police were put in charge of all crime, including political crime. As Robert O. Paxton, the finest historian of Vichy France, wrote, "The logic of the armistice poison thus drew Vichy into trying to do the Germans' dirty work for them." Sometimes the work was dirtier than even the Germans demanded: sending Jewish children to their deaths was a French initiative.

That France seemed to have been given more freedom than other occupied countries was simply a great convenience for the Germans. Their troops, assigned to relatively light Occupation duty thanks to a soon-enlarged French police force, were available for battle in the East, and the Germans benefited from an obedient French government, huge payments for Occupation indemnities, and raw materials and labor that were cheap against a new, and highly unfavorable, exchange rate. Pétain, comfortably tucked away in Vichy, 195 miles south of Paris, was more than compliant, and the word patriotism was stretched by all sides to the point where it made no sense. "I used my power as a shield to protect the people," Pétain told a judicial inquiry after the war. "I paved the way for Liberation by preserving France, suffering but alive."

It was not a time for heroics, because the worst possible thing had already happened to the French: their belief in themselves was shattered. In the Battle of Britain spines stiffened, in France's war they slumped. England loves itself in adversity, France loves itself in majesty and there was none left. The French became both victims and accomplices, their one aim to see that life went on, whatever that meant.

"Abandoned populations—put your trust in the German soldier," said a poster showing a handsome soldier enfolding a small urchin in one arm and with the other offering a biscuit to a child clinging to his knees. The

Occupation troops were carefully chosen, especially for Paris. They were neat and mannerly, and the word still used about them ad nauseam is "correct."

"The one thing we learned in four years of Occupation is that the German is correct," Jean Dutourd would write in his savage black market satire, *Au Bon Beurre.* Their hair was so well brushed, their boots were so well shined, their respect for French culture was so affecting. Speaking of a German soldier over lunch at Florence Gould's, Marie-Louise Bousquet told the ineffably correct writer and officer Ernst Jünger, "With a regiment of young men of his caliber the Germans could have conquered France without firing a shot."

With all of France's riches to plunder, the Germans made their first major move on, of all things, the haute couture. The entire fashion industry, including its workers, would be transported to Berlin.

It seems to me that, in Nazi logic, it was a perfectly sound choice. High style was lacking, and the easiest thing was to appropriate it from France just as Göring took the paintings he fancied from the Jeu de Paume museum. The idea was not frivolous: Magda Goebbels and Emmy Göring and wives of other high officials and ambassadors had to be able to embody the culture and taste of the Third Reich as it took over the world.

The fashion takeover began in late July, within weeks of the armistice, when five German officers entered the offices of the Chambre Syndicale de la Haute Couture, high fashion's governing body, questioned the general secretary,

Daniel Gorin, who replied with caution, and then left with the files of foreign buyers.

A few days later, a Sunday, the Germans broke into the offices and removed almost all the remaining files and archives. In August, the couturier Lucien Lelong, head of the Chambre Syndicale, was informed of the fate of the French haute couture: it was to disappear. Designers and their staffs would be transferred to Berlin or Vienna (which had a more fashionable past than Berlin), and Paris would lose an unfair monopoly that did not correspond to the needs of the New Europe. Lelong replied, "Haute couture is French or it does not exist," and told the Germans that fashion creativity cannot be stolen since it springs from cultural traditions.

Lelong owned a successful house whose well-bred clothes were produced by a team of designers that included Pierre Balmain and Christian Dior. "He dressed women very well, nothing extraordinary but in good taste and well-made," said Florette, who admired him. More significantly for dealing with the Germans, he was the one designer who was also part of Paris society, according to Prince Jean-Louis de Faucigny-Lucinge, an infallible arbiter of such things. Even Chanel, always welcome at fancy dress balls because she was amusing and wore wonderful costumes, would not be invited to private dinners, something she understood and accepted perfectly well. "There was a social custom that one did not entertain one's tradespeople," she told the journalist Marcel Haedrich. Lelong came from a gentlemanly background and, above all, was married to a beautiful and very mondaine Russian princess, Natalie Paley. His social standing, of which the

Germans were surely aware, helped make him a formidable opponent.

Using his connections, Lelong quite simply saved the haute couture. His first act was to enlist the press and radio in a campaign to show the cultural importance of French fashion, a move that cut across political lines. As Germaine Beaumont, a dowdy but influential author, wrote, "It may be just a dress but it is the entire country that created it."

Lelong's next step was to show that the loss of the couture would be an economic disaster for France and therefore for Germany: not only would the great houses be gone but a legion of small suppliers of buttons, trimmings, feathers, and embroidery would be out of work. On the other hand, keeping the couture in France meant the possibility of earning a great deal of foreign currency from neutral countries in exchange for very little raw material. "Before the war," he argued, "it was calculated that one exported haute couture model enabled us to purchase ten tons of coal."

Summoned with Daniel Gorin to Berlin, Lelong did not let up. And eventually the Germans backed off, convinced that the couture would break down on its own under draconian rationing and constant harassment. It was awarded a so-called state of exception, which was then called into question no fewer than fourteen times (both Balenciaga and Grès were briefly shut down, then allowed to reopen). "More than once observers were sent from Berlin who demanded that the collections be shown to them," Lelong wrote, "but it was never possible to discover the exact nature of their mission."

Vionnet had retired and Mainbocher, an American, and Molyneux, who was British, left France, as did Schiaparelli, whose house remained open so that her workers would not be out of jobs. Chanel, who had shut down her couture activities to move to the Ritz with a German lover, kept her perfumes going so that she could seize back the rights she had sold to the Wertheimer brothers, who, as Jews, were now in exile. She failed on a legal technicality. Marcel Rochas, who dressed the wife of Prime Minister Pierre Laval, crossed the street rather than greet his Jewish former clients; pretty blond Jacques Fath and his pretty blonde wife, Geneviève, became ornaments of what were politely called Franco-German gatherings.

The remaining houses were limited to thirty (more were later added) and their fabric consumption was cut to 50 percent of what it had been before the war. Each collection could show only 100 models, reduced to 60 by 1944, with yardage strictly regulated according to the kind of models—suits, coats, day dresses—shown.

Just as Lelong's efforts remain largely unsung outside the trade, so fashion historians tend to ignore the influence of the new sumptuary laws on styles during the Occupation. If Balenciaga, for example, showed few evening gowns, it was because from 1943 they could be sold only to actresses. If he used more lace and embroidery, it was not, as has been suggested, because of a Goya influence but because it had been decreed, in 1942, that in order to keep the smaller artisans in work, each collection had to include at least one model containing, or entirely composed of, lace. Embroidery was to be used on 10 percent of all models and two of them had to consist entirely of embroidery. It was not a situation likely to encourage creativity, but it kept 97 percent of the couture workforce in their jobs.

In order to be a customer a woman had to hold a couture card (15,016 were issued in 1942), which was given in exchange for two hundred francs and two kilos of fabric. Another two hundred cards were allotted to the German authorities. Contrary to belief, couture customers during the Occupation were almost all French (German officers had for the most part left their wives at home), which accounts for the small number of German cards. Since couturiers, including Lelong, were obliged to receive all card-carrying customers, the clientele was a new mix. There was plenty of French funny money around, profiteers from sales of seized Jewish property and black marketers known as BOFs, from *beurre, oeufs, fromage*, the commodities so many of them dealt in.

One couturier sold four dresses to a rather gross woman from whom, on his service staircase, he had earlier bought butter at the exorbitant price of three hundred francs a kilo, and, peering through the curtain one day at Lelong's, Christian Dior said to his friend Pierre Balmain, "Just think! All these women are going to be shot wearing Lelong dresses!"

There were questionable clients at Balenciaga, too, although the BOFs, while impressed by his high prices, generally preferred the showier clothes of someone like Fath. Marie-Louise Bousquet dropped by, of course—"she was not very appreciated by us," Florette said—and while Florette's order book shows no German names, most of the clients were new: the mistresses (sometimes titled) of German officers and the wives of Vichy government officials. Many of the Rothschilds had gone to New York, where the Baroness Alain dressed at Hattie Carnegie and received, she never knew how, the occasional hat from her Paris milliner, including one with a sweeping green feather that she happened to wear on Saint Patrick's Day. "They thought I was Irish," she said.

The house of Balenciaga was, like the rest of Paris, too quiet, too expensive, and too cold: after the war Carmel Snow's fitter apologized for the slowness of her chilblained hands. Clients had to climb three flights of stairs since the elevator was shut down, but still they came. "So many houses were closed and Balenciaga was much in demand," Florette said. By 1943, when the war was at its worst, her sales, bolstered by high prices, surpassed those of 1938. Clients ordered slacks for country or home use, culottes for bicycling, fur-lined hostess gowns, and an outfit called a *bain de soleil*, a halter-necked playsuit for women who were in the unoccupied south of France and at play. Wladzio d'Attainville, his military service over with the French defeat, made huge hats to balance austere outfits until the authorities banned hats as a waste of material and Balenciaga called in the hairdresser Guillaume to build big chignons padded with a piece of stuffing known as a rat. Florette wore her rat as a false beard to one of the Saint Catherine's Day parties but lost it when she put it on a table in order to drink an ersatz orangeade. Thereafter, and for the rest of her Balenciaga career, she scraped her hair back into a tight chignon *à la banane*.

She bicycled to work in a brown corduroy culotte suit that she exchanged upstairs for her black vendeuse dress. Sometimes clients with country houses would bring a precious gift of food; sometimes she went with Maria, the rackety Spanish vendeuse, to a bar on the nearby Rue

Boccador where one could pick up a bit of butter or a black market egg. "So I had to go out drinking with her and when I came home my husband was glad but said you're picking up bad habits." The rule of the times, she says, was to say nothing and think nothing. "It was a question of work," she finally said one day when I had asked one question too many. "It may seem strange to you, but it was easier to work with the occupier than against."

In the only interview he is known to have given, a year before his death, Balenciaga brought up the attempted German takeover: "You know that Hitler wanted to transfer the haute couture to Berlin. He sent six enormous Germans—much taller than I—to talk about it. I said he might as well take all the bullfighters to Berlin and try and train bullfighters there."

His reply sounds a bit sassy for someone so circumspect, but since he once told Givenchy, who had suggested that he had exaggerated something, "You must remember, my dear Hubert, that I have never in my life told a lie," we must take the words as said. What is certain, if never acknowledged, is that the war years made Balenciaga into the great couturier he became.

His unusual situation as a Spanish citizen in occupied Paris meant that he could travel to his couture houses in neutral Spain and bring back fabrics that, although less good than those of prewar France, were better than what was available.

Another advantage was the continued publicity he got in the American press. French *Vogue* had closed down, so there was no Paris fashion news, but in the United States *Vogue* and *Harper's* were able to publish the occasional

Balenciaga design from Madrid. In 1941, *Vogue* described his "Drapery from Spain" and reproduced, with a half-page drawing by the leading illustrator, Eric, four models from the Barcelona branch that had been bought by I. Magnin in California. In 1944 *Harper's Bazaar* showed his hats with the caption "Extravagance in Madrid."

The third benefit, and the most crucial to his development as a designer, was, quite simply, the silence of those gray years. Closed off in his studio, which became a sort of laboratory, Balenciaga could work quietly and develop his craft. Until then he had merely been gifted: by war's end he was unique. Every scrap of fabric, no matter how synthetic and shoddy, became a subject of study. From this came his unequaled mastery of construction and his fanciful use in later years of embroidery and trimmings—the curly green plumes of ostrich feather on an evening coat, the cabochon pearls Lesage made for him in 1964, the black jade on brown lace, the swirls of chenille, the snowflake effect of a huge guipure lace evening cape, the expert trimmer Judith Barbier's cascade of pink and white flowers made from parachute silk—all had their beginnings in the strictures of wartime Paris. Technique fully mastered, he was free to dazzle and to dare.

When I asked Florette if, in addition to fabrics, Balenciaga ever brought back from Spain foods that were unobtainable in Paris, she replied, "He never gave me any, though once when I was in bed for a month with internal bleeding caused by a lack of vitamins, he brought me some lemons. I thought that was very kind. He needed me, but still it was kind."

Like other neutral capitals in wartime, Madrid was

lively and luxurious, with the Allies and the Germans vying for Spain's support—glamorous spies (including, reportedly, Chanel for the Germans and the actor Leslie Howard for the British); Archbishop (later Cardinal) Francis J. Spellman on a friendly visit from New York to Franco; a screening of *Gone With the Wind* at the American embassy (the French didn't get to see it until after the Liberation); and, from 1943, a fashionable branch of Horcher, the best restaurant in Berlin. Unseemly, yes, but so gay.

One day I dared ask if she thought Balenciaga had collaborationist sympathies, and it was the only time I saw Florette cross. "You simply do not understand," she said.

She was right. I did not, and do not, understand the period and am not sure that anyone can who did not live through it. I do not understand how it is that during years of asking I have never found a Parisian who, on two sunny July mornings in 1942, noticed fifty city buses carrying 13,152 Jews, guarded by French police, to their eventual destruction. And I do not understand, although I have searched the official archives, who Florette's client Mme Kiraly really was and what happened to her.

Mme Kiraly was a beautiful blonde—"rather like Grace Kelly," Florette recalled. She spoke French with a slight accent (the name is probably Hungarian), was awfully nice, and first appeared at Balenciaga on September 13, 1940, to order a fur-collared coat, a beige suit, and a black chiffon dress. She came back on September 27 for another number, and became a regular and frequent customer. On December 15, 1941, she asked to have riding breeches made, one pair for a boy and one for a girl—to my mind they were for the children of the German officer who was probably keeping her—and the orders came regularly until October 28, 1943, when she brought in a white coat and four suits to be refitted. She never picked them up.

A few months later, when Florette applied for a travel permit to go skiing, she found herself under arrest. She sent word to M. Bizcarrondo, who learned that Florette had been taken because her name figured in Mme Kiraly's address book. When the police were told that Florette was just a vendeuse, she was released. Mme Kiraly was never heard of again.

Florette believed she must have been a secret agent for the Allies. She thought Mme Kiraly had probably been taken to 93 Rue Lauriston, the notorious torture center of the so-called French Gestapo, a bunch of jailbirds who not only helped the Germans in their filthy work but also dealt in gangland trafficking and blackmail. Their specialty was an early form of waterboarding—"the place with the bathtubs," Florette called it, and shuddered.

All Parisians knew about, and were terrified by, 93 Rue Lauriston, a pockmarked brownish building near the Trocadéro. So notorious is the address that as recently as 2009 there was a failed attempt to change the house number from 93 to 91 bis. As if that would make a difference.

By 1943, when the Rue Lauriston was at its malign height and Mme Kiraly disappeared, the tide was changing for the Germans, and for Vichy, which simply meant that life became harsher, reprisals more cruel: the hands of the authorities became heavier as their nerves frayed. The effect on Parisians that Lee Miller noticed a year later on returning to Paris after photographing the war for *Vogue* must already have been evident: "The mental malnutrition of the past four years has sapped their strength. They are overdosed with self-preservation and underfed with self-sufficiency."

But how to be self-sufficient when everything depends on red tape and standing in line and when everyone is watching everyone else? When propaganda newsreels were shown in cinemas, the lights were brought up to deter anyone from whistling or booing or simply reacting. The Germans set back Paris clocks to run on Berlin time and everything felt slowed down: so many hours had to be spent on the business of daily life.

Shoes were the greatest clothing problem, since there was no leather and even a repair required a coupon. Varieties of wooden platform soles were introduced, the most flexible being a German import with the unfortunate name of Smelflex. "The entire gait of the French woman has changed with her footwear," Lee Miller noticed. "Instead of the bouncing buttocks and mincing steps of 'pre-war,' there is a hot-foot long stride, picking up the whole foot at once."

Since only one hairdresser in Paris had dryers (the heat being generated by sturdy young men on stationary bicycles), women wore turbans or pompadours, with their hair trailing in the back. They were doing their best but looked so strange that an odd theory grew up: Frenchwomen had uglified themselves to mock the enemy. Some of the very young, the so-called *zazous*, accessorized wildly, and with victory in sight there was a move to mocking extravagance despite restrictions, but the theory is nonsense—there isn't a Frenchwoman alive who would choose to be seen at a disadvantage—even though it became an enduring myth.

Christian Dior wrote in his memoirs that wartime styles "originated in a desire to defy the forces of occupation and the austerity of Vichy," while a respected British historian adds, "During the Occupation, even Communists had regarded Parisian fashion as a weapon of Resistance." Thus the Parisienne, born to preen, became a heroine of sorts, and when Dior invented his extravagant New Look in 1947 he made a point of saying it was a reward for her wartime sacrifice.

Among the beau monde, the constraints were fewer. Florence Gould and Marie-Louise Bousquet entertained usefully and parties went on with some changes in cast. The butler of Robert de Rothschild, whose house had been requisitioned for a Luftwaffe general, said to Jean Cocteau, "I am not unhappy here with Monsieur le Baron, I mean General Hanesse. He receives the same people as Monsieur le Baron." German repression was sometimes a thrill. Young Philippe Jullian, a would-be writer up from the provinces and making a splash with his drag impersonations of society ladies, noted the plus side of the curfew: "People arrested after its expiration were taken to police headquarters to spend the rest of the night. Many people who didn't know each other made contacts that were pleasant and useful."

The Duchesse d'Ayen, from French *Vogue*, went to 93 Rue Lauriston to try to find her kidnapped husband, who was locked in the basement, although no one told her. He died in a German camp and she spent several months in solitary confinement in Fresnes prison wearing the beige jersey Balenciaga dress she was arrested in. Other society ladies "resisted" by speaking French with a British accent

when chatting with German officers. Marie Laure de Noailles, with her wildly transgressive gene pool, as usual did
as she pleased. Her father had been an immensely rich
Jewish banker, while her mother was descended from both
Proust's model for the Duchesse de Guermantes and the
Marquis de Sade and was the first woman to say *merde* in
polite society.

One morning, two men whose raincoats and dark hats
identified them as French Gestapo came to Marie Laure's
sumptuous mansion on the Place des États-Unis. She received them in bed: "Gentlemen, has no one told you to
remove your hat in a lady's bedroom? Emma, bring me
my tea."

Finally, on August 25, 1944, Paris was liberated and everyone, except for those who had reason to hide, united in
its explosions of joy. The Noailles had lunch at home with
the Faucigny-Lucinges and, having first closed the shut-
ters against the noise, went out to join it, catching a glimpse
of the politically elastic Jean Cocteau as he waved victori-
ously from a tank. Florette and Payot bicycled to the Place
du Trocadéro to celebrate; Balenciaga invited the Bizcarrondos and Pierre Balmain to dine with him and d'Attainville
in their flat on the Avenue Marceau, where they listened to
the bells ringing all over town and heard "La Marseil-
laise" sung for the first time in four years. "The victory
would efface our old defeats," Simone de Beauvoir wrote.
"It was ours, and the future it opened was ours, too."

"It is not that France had behaved the worst. It is that
France mattered the most," the historian Tony Judt wrote

of the defeat. And so it was for the liberation: there were other cities that had suffered more or that were more strategic, but Paris mattered the most. The news of its liberation set church bells ringing from London to Mexico City. Parisians were scarred, some forever, but the city was miraculously intact under blameless blue skies: there was every reason to celebrate, and everyone did.

And yet the autumn and winter following the liberation were in many ways the harshest as the war continued in Europe. Bread rationing came back—rationing in general continued until 1948—and there were power cuts, no buses, and no shoes, even with wooden soles. The New Year's message from the minister of the interior was grim: "1945 will be the hardest year of all, that of the final stretch."

But by October 1945, American *Vogue* was able to publish six whole pages of drawings of Paris fashions, even if the clothes themselves could not yet be imported, and six months earlier Philippe Jullian attended the Balenciaga collection: "A desire to applaud after each dress," he wrote in his diary. "One can imagine the joy of a Manet or a Whistler before such elegance."

Unmindful of conditions in Paris, *Vogue*'s Edna Woolman Chase cabled Lee Miller from New York to criticize the lack of elegance of her fashion reportage and wondered if Solange, Duchesse d'Ayen, in the Paris office couldn't find higher-class models—society ladies perhaps? Miller sharply replied that maybe the duchess, having lost her husband and only son, didn't have the heart to think about fashion shoots.

Bettina Ballard returned from service with the Red Cross to visit the duchess, who told her how, in solitary confinement at Fresnes, she had danced rumbas, tangos, waltzes, and even the Charleston to keep her circulation going although she had never been much of a dancer. The Balenciaga dress she wore and slept in for months had, she reported, been cleaned and looked very good again. Her russet hair, Ballard noted, had grayed and, if she seemed much smaller, her eyes were larger. "Looking at her I felt I was seeing a ghost," Ballard wrote.

French *Vogue*'s editor, Michel de Brunhoff, was likewise diminished, having lost his only son. Ballard made the rounds of couture houses, starting with Balenciaga, whom she had known from before the war. His salon looked dingy and there were strange customers paying in cash with big banknotes. They were black market wives, he explained with some distaste, buying at any price even models that were too small. Balenciaga himself, she wrote, "seemed very little touched by the war, or, for that matter, by the liberation. He wasn't at all surprised to see me there. As always, he led his own secluded life, busying himself with the only thing he really knew anything about—clothes."

Carmel Snow, worried about competition from *Vogue*, beat Ballard to Paris despite travel restrictions, having asked Louie Macy to get her husband, Harry Hopkins, to pull strings in Washington. Snow managed a circuitous route that took her via Caracas to Dakar to Madrid, where she had dinner with M. Balenciaga, as she still called him, and went with him to the flea market. She then took the train to Paris with a box of chocolates Balenciaga had given her, her only food on the twenty-four-hour trip. Snow's real friendship with Balenciaga, which she seems to have re-

Balenciaga with Carmel Snow

garded as a romance, only began in August 1946, when Marie-Louise Bousquet took her to dine in his apartment: "This was the first time I had really talked to Balenciaga— and how we talked! It was enchantment all around." They had no common language, Snow's French being merely confident and Balenciaga's English nonexistent, but her chauffeur, ordered for ten, had to wait until two in the morning.

As one combustible French government followed an other, the sole novelty in a ravaged world was the eruption of a new and, as it turned out, highly exportable intellectual wave, existentialism. Neither Jean-Paul Sartre nor Simone de Beauvoir was quite sure what people meant by the term, but they delighted in their celebrity. "I enjoyed seeing my name in the papers," Beauvoir admitted, "and for a while the fuss about us and my role as a 'Parisian figure' gave me a great deal of amusement." French intellectuals seemed the spokesmen for the age and once again, briefly, Paris was the cultural capital of the world.

Culture also meant couture, as it had throughout French history. As Beauvoir shrewdly explained: "Now a second-class power, France was exalting her most characteristic products with an eye to the export market: haute couture and literature."

Haute couture's move happened in the Chambre Syndicale, far from the cafés of St. Germain des Prés, when Lelong and Robert Ricci, son of the couturier Nina Ricci, dreamed up an improbable and triumphant scheme: a traveling show to display to the world the newest and best of French design. The clothes were shown on wire figurines 27.5 inches high in magical settings by top decorators, designers, and art world figures—Christian Bérard, Jean Cocteau, Boris Kochno, Emilio Terry, Georges Wakhévitch, Georges Geffroy—and the display was called Le Théâtre de la Mode. It opened the evening of March 27, 1945, in the Louvre's Pavillon Marsan as Allied troops were plunging into Germany, and it eventually toured through Europe and the United States.

The clothes displayed on Eliane Bonabel's wire figures were of astonishing precision and detail. Each outfit was made in exact replica of the collection's model—hand-stitched buttonholes that could be unbuttoned, real pockets, shoes, feathers, gloves, handbags that opened and were fitted with tiny mirrors, hats, and real hair coiffed by specially made minicurlers.

A Balenciaga, 27.5 inches
high, shown at Le Théâtre de
la Mode

The effort was intense, the quality amazing. All the
couturiers participated, and thanks to Bérard's artistic di-
rection the effect was hailed as pure magic, more indelible
than one would think. The Théâtre de la Mode was brought
back in another successful traveling show that opened
at the Louvre in 1990 and was the subject of an article in
American *Vogue* by Edmund White in 2006. What is left
of it is in a museum, Maryhill, in Washington State.

Its practical results were equally satisfying. Carmel
Snow and Diana Vreeland were photographed admiring
the exhibition in New York. At its opening, the *New York
Herald Tribune* said it spoke of "the heroism of a city that
in spite of terror and suffering saved itself, while preserving
alike its good taste, its loyalty to beauty, and its indefatigable

skills." More usefully for the export market, Tobe Coller Davis, in her influential Tobe Report, recommended that everyone in the retail and fashion business see the show: "Make no mistake about it—Paris is still the magic five-letter word."

Balenciaga contributed four models to the exhibition. There were more from Lelong, including two that seemed especially fresh and new. Although unattributed, they were by one of Lelong's assistants, and his name was Christian Dior.

3

After the celebrations, the hangover. Victory had been grand but life was threadbare and wan. Wartime restrictions dragged, shortages increased. Surely some relief was coming, was in fact deserved. "We felt we had a right to indulge ourselves," Pamela Churchill Harriman said later, and indulgence arrived precisely on February 12, 1947, in the midst of one of the coldest winters in history, with the first collection of Christian Dior. Skirts so full—twenty meters instead of the three that rationing required—that they knocked ashtrays off tables in the spanking new muted-gray salon; nipped-in waists and pert busts; the rustle of taffeta, which some of the younger fashion editors had never even heard; gracefully long hemlines: a flirty, pouty, enchanting artifice that was totally Parisian and thus universally admired. Dior had called his line Corolle, after the petals of a flower, but Carmel Snow, who knew something big when she saw it, gave it the name that endures: the New Look.

Never before or since has a fashion collection had such impact. It was denounced as wasteful and immoral; it required the wearing of painful waist cinchers, complicated fastenings, and a degree of fortitude when the wearer of a crinolined ballgown weighing sixty pounds attempted to dance. One woman made the long boat trip from Argentina simply to see the collection, and found the salon overheated. "I loved, loved, loved the New Look," the New York fashion editor Polly Mellen recalled many years later. Balenciaga was bemused: *What was Christian thinking of?* he wondered as he helped Bettina Ballard into a dress that had thirty buttons running down the back.

What Christian was thinking of, Dior explained in his memoirs, was happiness. His clothes were a reaction to the grim wartime years and his success, he felt, was because he brought back the neglected art of pleasing. "The prime need of fashion is to please and attract," he wrote. Balenciaga had already shown the narrowed waists, rounded shoulders, and fuller skirts that helped define the New Look, but Balenciaga was not out to please.

Dior was by all accounts an adorable man who looked, according to Cecil Beaton, like a bland country curate made out of pink marzipan (Jacques Fath, seeing a threat to his flamboyant fashions, described him as resembling a notary from the provinces). He set the best table in Paris, dying, aged fifty-two, at a slimming spa in Italy from a lifetime's surfeit of dishes like baked oysters in béchamel sauce and beef filet layered with slices of melting foie gras. He had led a happy sunlit childhood in a much-loved and ugly mansion in Granville in Normandy, the son of a fertilizer tycoon, one of France's richest men until he lost it all in 1931, and of a very loving mother. He was incurably nostalgic all his life.

Balenciaga's nostalgia, if indeed he had any, could not

be based on dappled trees and starched housemaids and soft settees. Growing up in a humble village where fishermen faced the threat of sullen seas, where women wore black and the local church, oversized and dark, spoke of duty and sorrow, he may have had that one enlightening encounter with the marquesa in her lovely Drecoll (or Redfern or Worth), but his was a harsh and rigorous childhood that left no room for misty memories.

Perhaps a tough start can be liberating. It must mean something that the three most radical couturiers of the twentieth century—Vionnet, Chanel, and Balenciaga—were the only ones to be born poor. They were driven and bold, not raised among genteel niceties, and thus free from the constraints of bourgeois habit and tradition. Unlike them, Dior was not an innovator, nor did he see himself as one. In his own words he was a reactionary, looking back to re-create gentler days. Born in 1905, Dior wrote, "I thank heaven that I lived in the last years of the Belle Époque. They marked me for life."

As a young man, his parents having denied him what they considered an ungentlemanly career in architecture, Dior took up undemanding studies in political science, which allowed him playtime with the brightest artistic figures in Paris—Cocteau, Bérard, the musicians of Les Six. He became a friend of Marie-Louise Bousquet, attended the better costume balls, including Louie Macy's, and opened a briefly successful art gallery when his father's finances failed. Having created costumes for the balls and for his friends' private revels, he sold designs to couture houses after the gallery closed, and before working at Lelong he found a job at the house of Piguet, where Carmel

Snow spotted and remembered his "Café Anglais," a light herringbone wool dress with a schoolgirlish lace trim. By the time Dior went out on his own, not only was he a friend of *le tout Paris*, but Ballard and Snow had marked him as someone to watch.

After the war, Dior and Balmain decided to leave Lelong and open their own house. But Dior dithered and Balmain went on alone with six hundred thousand francs. Dior, on the other hand, was brought to the attention of Marcel Boussac, who gave him a terrific contract and six million francs in backing—ten times what Balmain started off with. That Boussac was a textile and press tycoon may be thought to have helped, especially in a time of fabric shortages, but Dior maintained this was not so. He always said that he was exceptionally lucky and used a bunch of astrologers to ensure that this continued, unfortunately failing to heed their final advice, which was not to go to Italy to diet. After his death, his otherwise hard-nosed business manager told Japanese television that it was because God needed Dior to dress His angels.

Planning his maison de couture at 30 Avenue Montaigne, Dior knew exactly what he wanted—Louis XVI as revisited in 1910, he said. His decorator friends helped create an enchanting jewel box with soft colors and toile de Jouy and vast bouquets by Lachaume and, later, by Paule Dedeban. From the start he chose a team of five confidants including technical staff (he sketched delightfully but was ignorant of technique); his in-house muse, a woman of uncertain origins and implacable chic named Mitza Bricard; and—this was a first—an American PR man. The buzz was well prepared (Dior is said to have exempted eighteen top buyers from entrance fees) and so intense that *Life* magazine wrote him up before he opened. The day, despite the cold, a newly announced cut in the bread ration, and newspaper and garbage strikes, was a triumph such as no one, least of all Dior, had imagined. Within days, a crusty old member of the Jockey Club was complaining that in forty years as a member he had never heard the name of a couturier mentioned but now *on ne parle que de Dior.* By 1949 the house of Dior provided 5 percent of France's export revenue.

Dior stuck a flower in his lapel, hired a masseur, and went to the United States, where he delighted interviewers by showing them his good luck charms and was in turn thrilled when an immigration officer asked him where hemlines were going. No one until 1947 had paid much attention to hemlines, which suddenly became a worldwide obsession—"We waited each year for the announcement from Paris regarding next year's hemline," says a study of what ordinary Americans wore in the 1950s—that died only in 1970 when *Women's Wear Daily* declared everyone would wear the midcalf midi skirt and no one did.

Dior was the man. Within months of his first collection he had signed with a stocking manufacturer, and Dior neckties, which he had never seen but which bore his name, were sold at B. Altman and Company, the fusty New York department store. Before long, his franchise extended to five continents and the house of Dior had exploded couture into the branding device that today gives us such curiosities as the YSL dual voltage travel plug and a fishing rod by Chanel.

As for his clothes, Chanel herself said he made women

look like stuffed armchairs. Balenciaga said nothing and was among three thousand mourners at Dior's funeral in 1957, but he could only have hated the restricting hourglass shapes, skirts stiffened with horsehair instead of being skillfully cut to the desired fullness, and the idea that each season must produce a marketable different look instead of evolving from the last.

Dior himself said that Balenciaga was the conductor and that other designers were mere members of the orchestra. Admiring a suit of Bettina Ballard's, he told her it was so well made that it had to be by Balenciaga. "If only I were Balenciaga," he once said and probably meant it, sort of, in that he envied the hush in which Balenciaga worked.

The two men were not competitors: they had so little in common that they had no need to see each other as rivals and they shared such friends as Mitza Bricard, who did some of Balenciaga's hats. Dior was the decorator, Balenciaga the builder; Dior couldn't do what Balenciaga did, Balenciaga couldn't be what Dior was. Florette says that although no Balenciaga employees had been to Dior because they were banned from visiting other houses, they considered Dior a *maison snob*, by which she meant it was the latest house where everyone went, including Balenciaga's customers. Dior lent or gave dresses to people who were *en vue*, which Balenciaga refused to do. Dior eagerly courted the press; Balenciaga never even had a press attaché.

At Balenciaga collections, *Vogue*'s Susan Train says, there was a cathedral hush while at Dior the conversation level rose when customers' interest flagged. Dior was social theater, Balenciaga was serious stuff, says the writer and lecturer Rosamond Bernier: "His girls were often hideous, one was alarmingly wall-eyed, and they were told to look over the heads of people. At Dior, even early on, it was much more of a circus with everyone smoking furiously."

Early Dior was irresistible, and if Florette's sales remained steady, the earnings of the house of Balenciaga suffered from the New Look. The greater damage was to Balenciaga's pride, according to Hubert de Givenchy. "When the New Look came in he went to Mademoiselle Renée, his directrice, and said I haven't seen Madame X or Madame Y and Renée said Monsieur, they have gone to Dior. And he said, after all the trouble I have gone to they don't even come by for a dress or two. It was his Spanish side. He said that's it and he never again went into the salon to receive clients. People wonder about his mysterious side—that is the simple reason."

The reason wasn't quite that simple, although one can hardly expect Givenchy to mention it. Within a year of the New Look, on December 14, 1948, Balenciaga had suffered the greatest blow of his personal life when his longtime lover Wladzio d'Attainville died suddenly, aged forty-nine, in Spain. Dapper, charming d'Attainville had teased Balenciaga out of his shell and given him confidence. He made clever and amusing hats to enliven the sober dresses, he circulated in the salon and chatted to clients, his mother was photographed by Horst looking immensely distinguished ("Balenciaga," said the caption, "designs at-home clothes especially for her"), he was amusing and *mondain.*

To this day, Florette says, no one is aware of the almost seismic impact of d'Attainville's death: "If he had lived, the house wouldn't have been so serious, it wouldn't have had that weight. There was no one to lighten it up.

Monsieur Bizcarrondo wasn't capable of chatting to clients, I told him he should show himself more but he wouldn't. Nor would his wife." Devoted friends, if not socialites, the Bizcarrondos never left Balenciaga's side during the first dreadful shock and found him a replacement companion, twenty-three-year-old Ramón Esparza, a pleasant and good-looking Spaniard with a cleft chin who worked with Balenciaga in the studio, made hats, and stayed in the background. "Esparza was very nice for Cristóbal, that worked out very well," Luc Bouchage, a longtime friend, said. "He was warm and kept things going. He helped him enormously at work." But no one could ease Balenciaga's grief.

That grief was terrible, so deep that Balenciaga decided

Wladzio d'Attainville in the 1940s

The text on the placard reads:

Balenciaga
24 MAI 1949

67

Colette in the "collection of mourning"

to enter a monastery in Sully-sur-Loire and close his house. "It would have been a catastrophe," Florette said. "Everyone begged him not to because in the couture world it was like a beacon." Among those who begged were Balmain and Dior. According to legend, it was the sight of a client in a poorly executed Balenciaga that made him pick up his scissors again.

The result was a truly awful collection. "It was a collection of mourning, all black, sad beyond belief," Florette said. "We thought if that's the way it's going to be there's no point in going on." As it turned out, there was every point: his sorrow subsumed in his work, Balenciaga locked himself in his studio, and in the next decade he would produce the most brilliant clothes of his career.

By 1950 Balenciaga's spring collection was hailed as spectacular by *Vogue*, *Harper's* named him "the most elegant couturier in the world today," and he became a regular on the covers of both magazines. In *Elle*, Alice Chavanne scraped up as many factoids as she could about the mysterious stranger who was so secretive and distant, she said, that people asked did he exist, while Carmel Snow, who knew very well that he did, noted that the winter collection was the success of the season, with a five-minute ovation although "the monk of the couture still refused to appear." (Snow liked to use the word monk as shorthand to convey Balenciaga's reclusiveness and deep vocation; it also suggested that he was out of everyone's reach except, of course, her own.)

Balenciaga was no longer just a foreign dressmaker but

Balenciaga made French *Vogue*'s fashion map in 1948

couture. Fashion was ready for him, wanted him, needed his opulence and civility, for France was entering upon what the historian Jean Fourastié called *les trente glorieuses*, thirty years of a prosperity such as the country had never known.

In 1951 only one French household in twelve owned an automobile, and the Chelots, having acquired a second-hand Peugeot convertible, were among them (Florette says she was the first vendeuse to come to work in a car). They bought a small flat in the grand building on the Île St. Louis owned by Helena Rubinstein, a client, and where Mme Georges Pompidou, wife of the French president and another client, later lived. In their living room were a rather stiff portrait of Florette in a black jersey Balenciaga, a wishfully Louis XV commode from her mother-in-law's Callot days, and a smaller version of the carved wood gold sunburst clock that decorated Balenciaga's salon.

And then, M. Bizcarrondo having arranged easy credit terms, they bought their dream weekend house—*la maison du bonheur,* Florette called it—near the pretty village of Pacy-sur-Eure, on the route to Deauville: "All the people who'd spent the weekend in Deauville would stop by for a drink on the way back." Once when Florette was flaming some bananas (Payot usually did the cooking, and very well) she looked out the kitchen window and saw Balenciaga, who was out on a drive with Esparza, peering through the glass. "He was roaring with laughter at the sight of me at the stove." He was less amused by her larky plan to buy a motorboat and commute to work from the Île St. Louis. "Monsieur Balenciaga said it wouldn't do at all."

The 1950s seemed to have taken place on a sunny afternoon, the writer and critic Elizabeth Hardwick later said, and in Paris there was a sense of renewal and youth. Fresh blood was welcomed and enriched by the fact that prewar old blood was still around. In the space of one spring afternoon in 1951, the ambitious and beautiful young American composer Ned Rorem met Jacques Fath, Picasso, the costume designer Valentine Hugo, and Luis Buñuel. He had already met the composer Henri Sauguet, the writer Julien Green, Cocteau, Marie-Louise Bousquet and Marie-Blanche de Polignac, and later, with his patroness, Marie Laure de Noailles, he attended a Balenciaga collection where she noted approvingly of one particularly fragile gown, "I can see myself drunk in that one."

Even Balenciaga became relatively expansive and,

Sailor shirt, 1955

Suzy Parker by the Seine, Costume by Balenciaga, 1955 / Photograph by Louise Dahl-Wolfe

despite his aversion to being photographed, had posed for an advertisement for his perfume, Le Dix, named after his address on the Avenue George V. (His sculptural hand was placed, as it often was, in front of his slightly receding chin.) He went to at least one of the balls that started up again after the wartime hiatus—they were a useful guide to what women were wearing—and he was caught up in the web of Marie-Louise Bousquet, perhaps because she was inescapable and amusing, perhaps because he wanted to please Bousquet's boss, Carmel Snow. It was at one of her Thursday afternoons that he met the English director Peter Brook and his actress wife, Natasha Parry.

Bousquet had glommed on to the Brooks at once as the brilliant new couple, he a boy genius in London and the director in Paris of a pleasingly scandalous production of Genet's *Le Balcon*, she a beautiful film star. "It was a time when Noël Coward called us dreamboats—we would get

Balenciaga's sketch of La Reynerie, with blouse design at right

postcards Dearest Dreamboats," Natasha Parry recalled, laughing. They were also a lot more than mere dream-boats, and Balenciaga caught that at once and did something remarkable and grand. On that first meeting, with the shy person's sudden boldness, he offered them the use of his country house, La Reynerie, near Orléans.

"He was someone fine and sensitive and quiet," Brook says. "The purity, the finesse of the human being—that was it. Somehow we met and somehow we became very friendly, but it wasn't in any way a sort of enthusiastic gushing friendship, it was just a refined meeting out of which he did this thing which they said had never happened, ever, he said why don't you come to my house, there's a manservant who will look after you and it's at your disposal and so we went for a week or so."

It was, Brook says, "the most beautiful house, everything exquisite, a beautiful green garden all around and everything impeccable, just high style."

"The long dining table, a wonderful cook, we just sat there and ate the best cheese soufflé and listened to Brahms, the first piano concerto," Natasha Parry adds. " It was like a fairy tale, so exactly what we longed for, so exactly. The walled garden and the beams . . . We sent Balenciaga the most beautiful present we have ever given anyone, ever, a Ming horse from Spink's in London."

They didn't see Balenciaga again as they commuted between London and Paris, but when their daughter Irina was born in 1962 he sent them an antique silver christening cup. When in Paris, Brook attended Balenciaga's collections as a necessary part of the arts scene: "I was very interested because there was this thing of the everyday and

then there was style, something that was endlessly changing, and a sensitive person, the couturier, would have a sense
of these invisible waves." What was changing, and what
remained, was endlessly interesting, he says.

"When we first came here from England this was a
Proustian world. It was highly attractive. It wasn't snobbery in the low sense of the word but it was—I remember
there's a line from Cocteau, *The Infernal Machine*, in which
Oedipus says to Jocasta something like 'Who can resist silver
and gold?'—and coming from England, from the roughness
of war, the good roughness of the war in that old-fashioned
England, here there was a living refinement. Quality and
charm, not as today an effete thing. The high social level
was enormously attractive and alive."

Not all was right in the world, but for a time it was a lot
righter than it had been. Balenciaga was at the top of his
game, his solitary work in his studio during the war having given him a mastery of his craft that no one could
equal, his hands so deft and swift (some people claimed he
was ambidextrous) that they could execute his wildest fan-
cies, and some would be wild indeed: the one-seam dress,
the no-seam coat, the uncanny four-sided "envelope" dress,
the impractical sweeping trains, the emphasis on a graceful back, rather than frontal, view. No one was ever so classic and yet so eccentric in the dictionary sense of being far
from the ordinary center.

He loved putting in pins, Florette said, and allowed no
one else to do so in his presence. To Chanel he was the *only*
couturier: "Only he is capable of cutting material, assem-
bling a creation and sewing it by hand. The others are
just designers." Temperamentally so different, Chanel and

The "envelope" dress

Balenciaga were close friends, until they weren't. They dined together at Allard, exchanged gifts, and talked a lot about sleeves. The sleeve was, as is well known, Balenciaga's obsession: everyone connected with the house remembers anguished cries of *la manga* and the awful sound of the master ripping one out at the last moment.

"The sleeve was a mania with him and always a problem," Florette said. "In those days the buyers came by ship and their orders had to be ready to leave with them, not on the next ship. Once I had a huge delivery and I saw he was taking apart the sleeves of a dress I had to ship that night. I said, Monsieur Balenciaga, you can't do this, they have to be there at six p.m. He said, they can't leave like this, and kept on working. I finally started to cry and he said I was bad-tempered—*et en plus elle a un mauvais caractère*—and kept right on pinning."

Balenciaga's sleeves were constantly rethought and re-sculpted; Chanel's never changed but were, he thought, well conceived even if she made things easy by using malleable soft tweeds for her jackets. (John Fairchild says he saw her draw blood with her scissors while fitting a sleeve on a model.) Her high, narrow armhole made the wearer look vulnerable and tender, which was pleasing to her clients since they were neither. The two friends fell out dramatically over an interview with Chanel in Fairchild's *Women's Wear Daily*, Givenchy says.

"Chanel did something very bad. She had promised John Fairchild that she and Balenciaga would be photographed together in the Bois de Boulogne or some such place. She said to him, Cristóbal, I'd like to have my picture taken with you. He replied, Coco, with pleasure, but it's just

one? *Women's Wear.* He said not on your life because, between us, he loathed *Women's Wear.* She found herself in a
bit of a jam with Fairchild so she gave an interview in
which she said nothing but horrors about Balenciaga, about
his homosexuality, how he knew nothing about women's
bodies which was why he dressed them as he did. Dreadful
things. Cristóbal, who didn't speak English, knew nothing
about it, but Esparza, who did speak English, read it to
him one day.

"Balenciaga, who was the most discreet of men and the
kindest of friends to Chanel, heard these ignominies, all
because he had refused a photo! I remember I went to have
lunch with him and he asked me over the telephone if I
had seen the article. No, Cristóbal, I said. I know you saw
it. Well, yes, I did. Is this your idea of friendship, not to tell
me about it? If I didn't, it was to spare you pain. But it was
for you to tell me. Well, you were told and at least it wasn't
I who told you. That wasn't very friendly of you, he said.

"So I go to lunch and I find Cristóbal in tears. How can
that have happened? The gifts we exchanged, the things I
did for her. He wept and wept and said, I am leaving for
Spain, I cannot bear such things. He went to Spain and
stayed a fairly long time."

Everything that Chanel had given him, including her
full-length portrait by Cassandre, was sent back. When she
died in 1971, Balenciaga went to her funeral (*Women's Wear*
photographed him), but Givenchy refused to accompany
him. "I asked him, How could you have gone? He said,
You know, in life there are things one must forget, the ills
that people have done to you. May she rest in peace, *paix
à son âme.*"

4

To a tough cookie like Chanel, Balenciaga's vulnerability seemed a weakness; his staff knew it was his strength. He was friable by nature and so they made his house into a cocoon where he could work undisturbed and they welcomed to the salon only those who were welcome. "We don't want women who are just curious," his directrice, Renée Tamisier, who had all the allure of a prison wardress, would say. Balenciaga's isolation and his prices—the highest in Paris—gave the house a reputation for exclusivity and snobbery, but Balenciaga himself, being one of nature's gentlemen, was by definition beyond snobbery, even if many of his clients and staff were not.

His newly enlarged and refitted premises weren't dainty in the Dior style and hardly welcoming to the casual passerby, but in their voluptuous austerity they were totally in keeping with the man and his house. The entrance was via the boutique, which was well set off from the street, with a black-and-white marble floor, pilastered walls, chairs where clients could await their chauffeurs, and showcases that were horizontal rather than upright so their contents could not be seen from outside. Flanked by

The boutique serves as the set for a fashion shoot

Chinese statues of two life-size bronze deer, a cordovan
leather elevator patterned on an eighteenth-century sedan
chair silently lifted clients to the third floor salon where
access was guarded by the scowling Mme Véra, who was
the house's trilingual bouncer, not too well washed in Florette's opinion, and who, along with the usually invisible
but omnipresent Mlle Renée, established the reputation of
the house of Balenciaga as a rude, high-hatting place. Beyond Véra, two rows of black-clad vendeuses—there were
eight by then—waited at their desks. Only one of them
smiled: Florette. This was such a rarity in the house that
the *New York Herald Tribune*'s Eugenia Sheppard dubbed
her "the smiling one."

Even the shop windows, decorated by Janine Janet,
gave no hint of commerce. Balenciaga forbade the display
of merchandise, with the result that Janet created sculptures for them that were in their way as ravishing and
original as Balenciaga's own work—mythical creatures
and fantastic figures called Le Parfumeur, Le Couturier,
or La Modiste. Her last one was called the Tower of Babel.

Janine Janet, born in Réunion, a French territory in
the Indian Ocean, and thus at home with materials not
usual for shop windows, such as shells and barks and
branches and old nails, was married to a painter, Jean-
Claude Janet, whose work had hung in the show windows
of Hermès. Annie Baumel, the brilliant window dresser at
Hermès, suggested in 1952 that she go to Balenciaga, which
she did, addressing herself to Mlle Renée, who ran everything. Mlle Renée gave her some bedraggled ostrich plumes
to stick in the window.

One evening, gazing disconsolately at her first window

from the street, Janine Janet was joined by a stranger in dark glasses who asked why she was using such moth-eaten feathers. Because she had no choice, she replied. "Just go tell them you want three dozen of their most beautiful ostrich feathers," he told her and identified himself as M. Balenciaga. He then took her for a coffee at Chez Francis, at the bottom of the Avenue George V, told her to see the collection so she would know what he was about, confided that he, too, detested ostrich plumes, and gave her free rein to decorate the windows as she pleased. "His two orders to

Janine Janet

her were that they should represent luxury and should not display any goods that were for sale," her widower said in their rambling third-floor walk-up in the unfashionable Tenth Arrondissement of Paris. Janine died in 2000.

A window designed by Janine Janet

Jean-Claude, who died at the age of ninety in 2008, kept all her old Balenciagas, including one that she told Balenciaga she had bought on sale. "You mean to say we have sales here?" he said, astonished.

Janine's work having become instantly fashionable (Cocteau had her design the costumes for his film *Le Testament d'Orphée*), the Janets entertained artistic Paris at small dinners where she cooked excellent spicy dishes. "Balenciaga was always lifting the pot lids and asking what she was making," Jean-Claude said. "One could enjoy oneself with Balenciaga. His conversation was usually about the couture and his clients, but not in a gossipy way. He knew nothing about art, though he did know antiques. He didn't travel but was interested to hear about where we had been."

Florette was friendly with the Janets but not part of their circle. She and Payot no longer had their martinis with Balenciaga, now that he had reached the heights, and Florette called him Monsieur, although she could always put him at his ease. "One morning I came in very early and there was Monsieur Balenciaga, in a hairnet. He was terribly embarrassed. I said don't worry, my husband's hair frizzes too, and he does the same thing." Payot's hair was short and very straight.

The working relationship between Balenciaga and Florette became even closer, a neutral film of familiarity, for Balenciaga, taking the place of intimacy. "He would criticize me for my gaiety because the house style was somber. But sometimes I could make even him laugh, although it wasn't easy. And people liked my gaiety, look at the results in my order book."

Those results came from very hard work and long hours. "Sometimes Monsieur Balenciaga and I were the only ones still there. I would be preparing dresses for the next day, checking appointments, doing my sums, and telephoning clients, which was important because at about seven p.m. they would be at home, resting and preparing for the evening. So I chose that time to call and say I saw Mme So-and-So and we spoke of you, all that sort of little blah-blah, it was part of my work, the other vendeuses didn't do that. It was very important to catch clients at a relaxed moment and maintain a real contact outside the Avenue George V.

"One night Monsieur Balenciaga came out of his studio and said, come in, I want to show you something. On the floor was a big piece of fabric, black crepe. He got on his knees, took out his scissors, and said, Florette, this is a dress we are going to present at the collection, which was two days later. There will be only one seam and it will be a dress you can sell to everyone." Barbara Hutton, her biggest client, ordered the dress in three colors.

It was Florette, with her sunny tact, whom Balenciaga ordered to eject a famous milliner and potential copyist from the collection ("he saw everything that went on in the salon through a peephole in the curtain"), as well as a woman who talked through the show. "But Monsieur, I can't make her leave," Florette replied, "she's one of our best clients." "Then just tell her to shut up," he said. And it was Florette who served as a guinea pig for what became one of his trademarks, the wide black satin belt with a large bow at the front, which in its first version was pink.

"The salon was full of buyers. He called me in and when he called you in you were always a little frightened because you thought you were in for criticism. He had a spool of pink ribbon next to him, he cut it, put it around my waist and made a marvelous bow. Then he opened the curtain. I didn't know what I was supposed to do so I took my courage into my hands and went to talk to my buyers and then I left. He wanted to see how it would look on an ordinary woman, not a mannequin, and he must have thought we'll see what Florette does."

He must have liked you very much, I said when she had told me this story. *"Sûrement,"* she replied. He clearly respected her eye, even when it disagreed with his. She never liked the saris he made in 1965 or the dresses that she called "too flamenco" and sometimes didn't even take numbers off their hangers to show to clients. "He knew about it and wasn't pleased. But I would say they are not for my clients."

Balenciaga had seen to it that Florette's desk was the one closest to the entrance to his private studio. Sometimes he called her into the studio. "It was never for a question of taste but to ask if a certain client liked this. He knew he could trust me. He would say, Florette's right, she's always right." The other vendeuses disliked her deeply.

And she disliked them all, with the exception of Odette Sourdel, the *seconde*, or assistant, of Lili, the only vendeuse, said Florette, one could talk to. "They all hated each other," Odette said, still narrow-eyed and sharp at the age of ninety. "It is not possible to get along when you are working on commission—it is a horrible way to make a living." She came to Balenciaga in 1948, family reversals having forced her to abandon her art studies. The name Balenciaga meant nothing to her, but because she spoke English

Ramón Esparza and Florette at a St. Catherine's Day party

she was hired two days before the summer collection. "Although I wanted to do it, it was very hard and I cried a lot."

D'Attainville publicly rebuked her for wearing flat heels, but Balenciaga, making a rare appearance at a Saint Catherine's Day party, came up to Odette where she was standing alone and said he had heard that he and a Basque friend of hers had the same ski teacher at Lech in Austria. "So he started talking to me about skiing while everyone stared." Except for Florette, she says, he didn't like vendeuses, rather grandly viewing them as living off his talent, which they were: "Maybe he spoke with me to avoid talking to them."

For a house that was considered the best managed in Paris, the vendeuses were rather a rum lot. Lili, who was Odette's boss, was Russian, a self-proclaimed royal. "Once she was talking about the Revolution with a client and said she had escaped thanks to her cousin. The client said, Oh Lili, we are related then. Lili completely lost it and burst into tears to avoid more conversation. One day she said to me, You know how to draw, make me a coat of arms. I asked, How? Just copy the Duchess of Windsor's crown with my initials, she said."

The duchess was Lili's client. Even Florette admits that Lili was a good vendeuse, though she despised her familiar ways: "She would sit down with clients," she said disapprovingly. She was shifty and odd, so why did Balenciaga hire her to begin with? "Because she spoke English very well," Odette said, "and because Russians were well thought of. Had she come from the Auvergne it wouldn't have worked."

(From left to right) Maria, Mlle Renée, Lili, and Florette

Each vendeuse had her system for snagging, or even poaching, clients. Sometimes Mlle Renée assigned them: it was she who gave Bunny Mellon, who in Odette's words bought mountains of dresses, to Alice, who was Renée's *petite amie*, though no one was supposed to know. Alice also had the Baroness Guy de Rothschild and Rita Hayworth.

The veteran vendeuse Marthe got Mona Bismarck, who had known her from her Paquin days. Maria, the friend of Balenciaga from Spain who had had a doomed affair with a toreador, had Marlene Dietrich. Margot, who inherited Mona Bismarck when Marthe retired, was not a good vendeuse, being lazy, and like the others was jealous of Florette's earnings and contemptuous of her willingness to work with mere manufacturers and buyers. "She said to me with all your running around you'll get blisters on your feet," Florette recalled. "I said it's better than getting them on my behind."

Some of the vendeuses thought the *premiers d'atelier* were just jumped-up seamstresses, wearing black dresses and pearls as if they were as good as vendeuses although, unlike the vendeuses, they had to use the employees' entrance. They were in fact a lot more powerful than the sales staff: it was best to stay on good terms with them to squeeze in clients, to get a rush job done, to persuade them to use their great skills on an unpromising body. Lili would go to the workrooms on Saint Catherine's Day with her guitar and sing Russian songs to the seamstresses; other vendeuses, says Florette, would tip the *premier* for quicker service. Denis, she said, was easily bought, although he was so grand that he was nicknamed the Emperor and was often mistaken for M. Balenciaga when he swanned in his white smock through the fitting rooms. "He would approach clients with scorn," Florette said. "I made fun of him but he worked extremely well."

There were ten ateliers, each holding between thirty and fifty workers. Three were for the *flou*—or soft—fabrics, five were *ateliers tailleur* for suits and coats, two were for hats. Each *premier* was also a fitter and had his or her own style. Florette would choose the atelier according to the client and the dress: "Some were very good, some gave a bit more, some were perfect but a bit dull." The favorite of Odette and Florette, and of Balenciaga, was Salvador, a very nice man who had trained with Balenciaga in Spain and had Courrèges and, later, Ungaro as assistants. "He

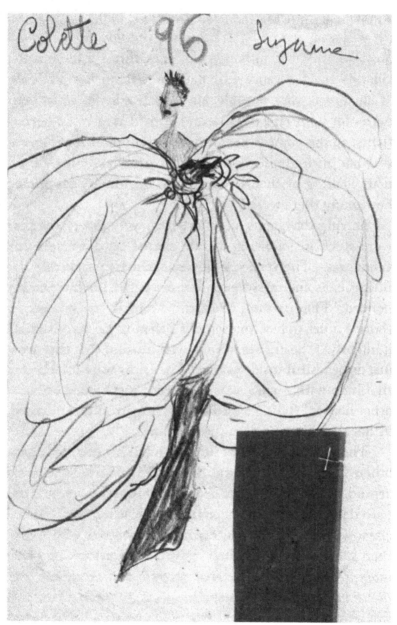

Workroom sketch with fabric swatch, 1951

worked very quickly and gave great chic to his clothes. Denis was a bit flat," Florette said. In the *flou*, Suzanne was quick and perfect, although she once threw a handbag at Odette's head because Lili had messed up her schedule. "Claude was very sensible, she had less style, which was better for some clients," Florette said. "Lucia was a perfectionist to the point of keeping clients on their feet forever, so I had to find clients who didn't mind standing for an hour looking at themselves in the mirror. It's surprising how many there were."

During the clients' fittings (there were three), the pins were stuck in following a code shared by the fitters and vendeuses. "The vendeuse never touched a pin during the fitting, but sometimes we could spot a defect the fitter hadn't noticed," Florette said. "You know how if you give something a quick glance you see more than if you have studied it intently." The dresses were so well finished that they were just as beautiful inside as out: "The hems were attached to the dress with a piece of chiffon, not just tacked on as at other houses." This gave an almost imperceptible rounded, rather than flat, finish to the hemline.

The ateliers worked in silence and didn't mix with each other. The lowest grade was the *arpète*, a fourteen-year-old errand girl with a magnet around her neck with which she picked pins up from the floor and then washed them. Balenciaga would hire only untrained seamstresses who would then laboriously work their way up the hierarchy: *petite main, seconde main débutante, seconde main qualifiée, première main débutante, première main qualifiée*. Once this was over the worker might rise to *second d'atelier* and then to *premier*. It could take a good twenty years, and even then not all the candidates were suited to dealing with clients. Those who seemed likely were sent to Balenciaga's Madrid house for two years so they could make their mistakes in private.

"Yes, it was a hard place, it was tough, but it was right," says Coqueline Courrèges, who joined Salvador's atelier as a *petite main* in 1951 and met her husband, André, there. "You punched the clock and if you were three minutes late, fifteen minutes were deducted from your paycheck. You had to be there, needle threaded, spools in place, ready to sew. One never dared open one's mouth, you had to understand everything with your eyes."

Coqueline Courrèges saw M. Balenciaga only once in her years working in his house. And she never saw a piece she had worked on in its finished state, not even on one of the house models. Nor did the other seamstresses. Florette found this intolerable and would invent an errand to get one of the girls, however briefly, to the fitting rooms. "There they were sewing with their aching backs and earning nothing, and it was their only chance to see a dress outside the atelier. It didn't take much to make them happy and I did it when I could. I could see it in their eyes and they would say, *Qu'elle est belle, ma cliente.* Because for that moment she became her client."

The carefully choreographed winter and spring collections followed roughly the same order at all the fashion houses, although only at Balenciaga were the ashtrays that viewers dipped their cigarettes in made of heavy marble. Suits and daytime dresses came first, then evening wear of increasing formality and almost transgressive luxury. To capture attention, which might wander during an hour-long show, Dior wrote in his memoirs that toward the middle of a collection shocking new models would appear: "it is the custom to call them the 'Trafalgars,' those which made the covers or full pages of the magazines." A Balenciaga Trafalgar might have been his glittering torero's jacket or a detachable pierrot sleeve with a pointed top. At every house, the collection closed with a floor-length bridal gown worn by a model looking as young and chaste as possible. And then the designer (but never of course Balenciaga) would take a bow.

By the time the clients have arrived, squabbles among their vendeuses to secure the best seats have been angrily resolved, the *premiers* have had their last-minute showdowns with M. Balenciaga (*la manga!*), and the staff has seen the night-before dress rehearsal and noted which numbers should be the great hits. M. Balenciaga is in a barely controllable state of nerves. And then out lope the mannequins, cool and indifferent in the finest clothes in Paris, languidly waving the outfit's number printed on a card or sometimes pocketing them, as if to suggest that actual selling is not the point. They are said to be the ugliest models in Paris.

I wonder about this, having spoken to Balenciaga models from the 1930s, the 1950s, and the 1960s, all of them very good-looking, even now. Some, it is true, had been chosen by Balenciaga simply because they resembled major clients (Givenchy called one of them "Moonface"), but the reputation for odd looks was probably due to the overpowering influence of Colette, still at work after nearly twenty years and still preceded by her lantern jaw as she flung the curtain open and crashed into the salon. "She had great authority and chic," Florette said. "She walked in like a grenadier, as if she wanted to kill everyone. The way she would come to a halt before clients! One was afraid. Poor thing, she was madly in love with Monsieur Balenciaga, she did everything she could . . ."

If Balenciaga kept his distance from the vendeuses and had endless technical quarrels with the ateliers, to the house models, who were as passive as sleepy kittens, he was benign. "If a girl fell ill he would send her a basket from Fauchon," says Danielle Slavik, a model in the sixties. It was a dull and indecently underpaid job: the girls had to clock in at nine and wait in the two models' *cabines* for the two-hour daily showing at 3:00 p.m. Before that, they might have a fraught fitting with M. Balenciaga, which could last for hours, or be called on by vendeuses to model an outfit for a client. Mostly they sat waiting, doing astrological charts and knitting. "They taught me how to knit," Florette said.

In the 1950s Balenciaga brought in a house model, Nicole Parent, who stayed only a couple of years because she had other fish to fry but who represented a new style for him: the sassy gamine. Clearly, although it was not something he would admit, Balenciaga must have been influenced by Dior's delight in Zizi Jeanmaire, and like her, Nicole was a dancer. She was in a popular revue and thought a bit of moonlighting would be fun until her show went on tour to the United States. She came from a good family (her brother was the architect Claude Parent, mentor of Jean Nouvel), and she wandered in to Balenciaga to see if she could earn pocket money as a model.

"When I came to that house, I said to myself, What an atmosphere, it's like a convent. I was in black, in a very tight suit and carrying a long umbrella, which was much done at the time. Alexandre did my hair and my face was covered in paint, like a stolen truck. I was sent to Véra, who sent me to Salvador, whom I adored. He laughed at the sight of me and then sent me to M. Balenciaga, who had me walk and said I would do. I didn't even know the dates of the collections, but he was about to start work on one."

The next step was Mlle Renée, who appreciated her dancer's discipline and was understanding about getting her out for curtain time. "But Florette was my sunshine," she said, "always gentle and kind." Nicole could—and still can in her eighties—get by on two hours' sleep, but sometimes she would curl up under a clothes rack for a nap. "Florette would say, Don't disturb her, we'll get someone else to show the dress." The two women remained friends well into this century, with Nicole in a pilot's leather helmet driving Florette to lunch at the Interalliée Club in her Morgan 4/4 sports car. (She also has a pilot's license and a black belt in judo, and she only gave up her splendidly customized Harley 883 at the age of eighty-one.)

With Balenciaga her relations were uniquely relaxed, even cheeky. "One day at a fitting I was sighing a lot and he raised his eyes and said, What is it, don't you like what I'm doing? I figured I had nothing to lose, so I said no. Dead silence, then he said, Why? Because it makes me look wider than I am tall and anyway I only like black. Me, too, he said.

"Another time he put me in a flowered dress—I hate that—in satin, with crossed straps in the back. He said, You don't like this one either—why? I don't like the fabric

Nicole Parent on her customized Harley 883

and I have shoulder blades that stick out so the straps won't work. He took that one away, too."

She even dared a joke during one of the last rehearsals before a collection. "We started at six and I had to be at the theater at eight. He knew it although it wasn't I who told. I was showing a suit with three-quarter sleeves and had forgotten the gloves. He said, Fetch the gloves, but I, in a hurry, just pulled the sleeves down to my wrists. He stared, then he started to laugh. He, whose sleeves had to be correct to the millimeter!

"After that, he only made me either very theatrical clothes or young things in cotton, not that I was the youngest but because of the way I moved, and he gave me a shorter hemline than the others." It was Balenciaga's first attempt at a youthful look, however constrained by the heavy elastic foundation garments he always made his models wear to ensure a smooth line. "It may be that I lightened up the place," said Nicole.

All was ready, then, for the collections to be seen, first by the buyers and the press, then by private clients. The salon—painted a nondistracting white, with gray carpeting—which comfortably held about thirty people, was stretched to its limits at collection time with the addition of the extremely uncomfortable little gold chairs that couturiers rented by the dozen from the house of Catillon.

The buyers, representing international clothing manufacturers and department stores, were the least desirable and the most rewarding: only at Balenciaga did they have to engage to buy, as an entrance fee, two outfits sold at a much higher price than private clients paid. But unlike the other houses, Balenciagas came in the appropriate fabric, not in muslin or in a paper pattern, and Balenciaga himself checked each one before delivery. The one thing orders lacked was the Balenciaga label, which, once the outfits were copied, usually in a cheaper fabric, and offered for sale, would say, for example, By Balenciaga for Saks Fifth Avenue. The money taken in from the buyers alone covered the cost of the collection; gains from private clients were pure gravy. According to *Women's Wear Daily* (August 1, 1959), Balenciaga had the highest net profit in the haute couture.

Some of the buyers were distinguished and mannerly; others, in their white neckties and pinky rings, were skilled thieves, secretly sketching details during the collections.

"It wasn't pleasant but one had to take away the paper,"
Florette said. "There was that peephole in the curtain and
Balenciaga always had his eye to it. He saw everything,
everything."

"The worst were the Italians," Odette said. "They
would send you off to look for something so they could be
alone with the dress. Buyers? They were just copyists."

The commissions Florette got from buyers' purchases
accounted for a large part of her excellent earnings. She
gamely dined with them or went to the Crazy Horse Saloon,
the new upmarket strip club oddly located next to Balenciaga, and she learned never to leave them alone with a
rack of dresses: "You know, those people were really very
gifted. You would show them a model and they would hold
up their fingers to measure the length or width of a collar.
Sometimes I said, Wouldn't you rather I just brought you a
tape measure?"

The big private clients, on the other hand, strode into
the salon as if half the world belonged to them, which in
many cases it did. They were not those Parisians who found
Balenciaga a bit too foreign but the international crowd
whom Truman Capote called Swans. Though they weren't
young, they had allure. God, Capote added, may have given
swans good bones but "some lesser personage, a father, a
husband, blessed them with that best of beauty emollients,
a splendid bank account."

Mona Bismarck, as she had recently become when she
first went to Balenciaga, was the most splendid of all. Born
in 1897, two years after Balenciaga, she had dressed at
all the great houses from Fortuny and Vionnet to Schiaparelli, who made her a dress in cellophane, and with her

third husband (there were five), the utilities tycoon Harrison Williams, was the talk of New York in the 1920s and 1930s. She was mentioned in a Cole Porter song ("What do I care if Mrs. Harrison Williams is the best dressed woman in town"—"Ridin' High," 1936), was named best-dressed woman in the world in 1933, and she made a total of fifty appearances in *Vogue* (one was a photograph just of her shoes).

During the Depression, which somewhat reduced Harrison's fortune of $680 million, the couple took what he called an "economy flat" in the Hôtel Lambert in Paris, one of the city's greatest buildings and later the home of the Baron and Baroness Guy de Rothschild. In their Fifth Avenue mansion, Mona's Christmas tree was hung with ermine tails to match the white walls.

When Mona came to Balenciaga, brought by Florette's client Barbara Hutton, Florette naturally hoped to capture her for herself, but she stayed with the elderly vendeuse Marthe, whom she had known at Paquin. "Mona was loyal, you know—once she found something she liked she stuck with it," Gore Vidal said. He became a close friend during her later years in Capri, where she gardened in terrific long linen shorts by Balenciaga fastened by an oversize button on the side. "She had the legs of a young boy," Vidal said.

Her body, lean and slightly androgynous, was like a perfect version of Balenciaga's favorite model, Colette. She was particularly suited to Balenciaga's satin hostess gowns with the wonderfully draped backs that Cecil Beaton emphasized in his portraits of her. The voluminous and grand hostess gown of the time was, of course, ideal swan attire:

Cecil Beaton's view of Mona Bismarck at home in Paris

Barbara Hutton, always the princess

Sable-lined Donegal tweed coat, 1962

Wool crepe daytime dress, 1968

Flounced gazar evening dress, 1965

ABOVE: Silk evening dress, 1965

OPPOSITE: Evening dress with trademark silk bow, 1966

Embroidery detail at neckline of previous dress

Embroidery by François Lesage, sweet peas by Judith Barbier, 1964

Daytime hat, 1950

it was worn only when receiving at home and indicated that the wearer was a cut above her guests since they were only passing through and the perfect setting they were dining in was all hers. Power dressing at its most refined.

With her shortish silvery hair, aquamarine eyes, and wonderful bearing, Bismarck had, Beaton suggests, an icy perfection. Like the Duchess of Windsor's? I asked Gore Vidal. "She had that side but she had that height," he said. "The duchess was smaller than anybody, she couldn't really make a great impression, except novelty. And she was funny, the duchess. Mona was droll, which is quite different. The stories that would come out . . ." He does not remember seeing her in her fabulous emeralds: "With those eyes, why wear them? It would be gelding the lily, as Darryl Zanuck would say."

There was nothing droll, or even funny, about Florette's major client, Barbara Hutton, the wasted Woolworth heiress who grew up motherless and with the taunts of underpaid striking Woolworth employees in her confused head. She was given to statements like "Look at the stars, they are free for everyone," spent, drank, and drugged prodigiously, was heedless but not unkind, and had so many husbands that for simplicity's sake Florette just referred to her as Princess except when she telephoned for a chat at four in the morning and Florette would gently remind her, "But Barbara, I have to get up and work."

In one day she ordered twenty-nine outfits from Florette, another day it was thirty-one. She had total recall of every collection and never needed to see a dress twice. The fittings took place in her second-floor suite at the Ritz, the grandest the hotel had, which was flanked by suites for her

ex-governess, Germaine ("Ticki") Toquet, and for Margaret Latimer, who had been her son's baby nurse. In the hall
were Vuitton trunks stamped with her various married
names.

"The fitters were Denis, whom she adored, and I also
gave her Suzanne because the orders were so big and Suzanne was so quick," Florette said. "We would arrive at
noon and spend the whole afternoon, Barbara drinking
from a glass of water, which was gin." For the great Beiste-
gui ball in Venice in 1951, Barbara had Balenciaga dress
her as Mozart at a cost of $15,000 (Yves Saint Laurent's *an-
nual* salary when he became chief designer at Dior was
$14,000). Balenciaga also made her a ballgown for that night
encrusted with jewels. It was so heavy she couldn't stand
in it, even when leaning on a chair, Florette said. She had
gone along to help, but not of course to go to the ball, spending the day at the Lido with Miss Latimer.

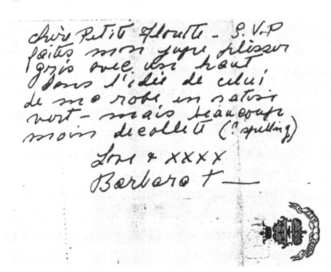

Barbara Hutton places an order

Another Hutton-inspired trip took Florette by train to Switzerland to bring her some of her emeralds for a ball to go with her green and white Balenciaga. "I had to get them from Cartier's safe—a huge necklace, a ring, earrings, a tiara. I was worried about customs so I told the conductor I had the flu and spent the trip in bed with the tiara in my handbag, the necklace under the covers, which I had pulled up to my chin, and wearing the ring."

Barbara clearly was fond of Florette and offered to buy her a house in the country: "She was rather hurt when I told her I already had one." They were born one day and one year apart and exchanged birthday presents, Florette usually receiving a Cartier pin and giving—"what do you give someone like that?"—a big bouquet from Lachaume.

"We are so much alike," Barbara liked to tell Florette. "We both lost our mothers young." She meant well but was unaware of the effrontery of saying that to an overworked woman with aching feet, and Florette, as she told me the story, seemed unaware of it as well.

For the most part, the clients were well behaved, and if they weren't, Florette set them straight, like the American woman she threw out and only readmitted when the woman's husband pleaded and gave her a crocodile handbag as a bribe. And then there was the infernal (Florette's word) Lady Roote, a motor tycoon's wife who used the pseudonym Lady Ann to throw customs inspectors in austerity Britain off the track and whom Florette also evicted. "One day I had enough and said go over to Givenchy, he has more time than I. She was back in ten minutes. To get there, which was just across the street, she'd had her chauffeur drive her in her Rolls."

I don't know how you could stand those people, I once said to Florette. "I don't know either," she replied, "but they could stand me. *C'est drôle, n'est-ce pas?*"

The newly rich with their barky voices were trying, but the solemn atmosphere of the house discouraged tantrums and in any case no woman, however spoiled, is at her best in her underclothes under the cool appraising gaze of a fitter and vendeuse. Florette was always smiling, giving confidence. It wasn't that all her geese were swans but she wanted them to look their best (and would be blamed by Balenciaga if they didn't). Florette liked steering clients and giving counsel. "It is odd because, even with people who knew exactly what they wanted, I always talked with them about why they wanted a particular dress. It's important to do that. The other vendeuses just wrote down orders."

The information she got was undoubtedly useful to Balenciaga and avoided such gaffes as the night when five women, including the Duchess of Windsor, appeared at a ball wearing the same Balenciaga. (None of them was Florette's client.) There were certain dress codes: one did not, and still does not, receive at home in a suit, which is only for street wear; an afternoon dress was often black, a cocktail dress more important and *recherchée*. Clients who could only buy one number chose black because showier dresses could only be worn two times, three at most.

Sometimes clients attended the collections with their husbands or lovers and the atmosphere could be pure Feydeau with someone like André Dubonnet skipping between past and present mistresses while prospecting for new ones. Florette enjoyed mildly flirtatious badinage—"none of the other vendeuses had so many men"—and was flustered only once, when she found herself in a fitting room with Rita Hayworth's glamorous husband, Aly Khan, helping him off with his trousers because he had lost a fly button.

"No one had as good a time with the clients as I did," she said. Once when she was awed by an English duchess— "the English are not easy to defrost"—Balenciaga said to her, "They are women, just like you. Be natural." She was, and her inborn friendliness enabled her to hit the right note between intimacy and service. "After all," she said to me one afternoon, "to a degree we were just ladies' maids. You had to remain somehow in the background. I was the vendeuse whom they thought of as perhaps more than a vendeuse, something of a friend perhaps. But I was not their intimate."

In the confines of the fitting room, however, she was. The Countess du Boisrouvray would sing "Frou-Frou" every time she tried on an evening gown and Florette would sing along with her, the two rolling their r's as one did in the Belle Époque. The daughter of the Bolivian tin magnate Simón Patiño, the countess went to Balenciaga every morning at eleven, and while she bought prodigiously, she didn't entertain a lot, according to her daughter, Albina, sometimes dining alone in her superb hostess gown. Albina, whose outfit of choice is jeans, says her mother was shy of Parisian society, though she duly gave a garden party each spring in her great town house on the Rue Perronet in Neuilly, paying the nuns who lived next door to pray for sunshine.

Florette's clients included Payot's old acquaintance the Begum Aga Khan and five or six Rothschilds, of whom her absolute favorite was the Baroness Alain de Rothschild, a sweet and beautiful woman who was painted by Balthus in a black Balenciaga coat. Over tea in her home with Florette long after Balenciaga closed, she fondly told me of taking her young son to Balenciaga, where Florette had five clients at once in five fitting rooms. "He noticed she had a different voice and a different manner with each of them. Pure theater," the baroness said.

The Baroness Alain was referred to as the Baroness Alain. Her sister-in-law Cécile de Rothschild, while also a baroness, was Mlle Cécile and just plain Cécile to Florette in the fitting room. Cécile was a tall, handsome woman with a brusque manner who sometimes came to fittings with her friend Greta Garbo, who bought nothing. "One day Cécile was saying Florette this and Florette that in her deep voice and Garbo said, You mustn't use that tone with Florette, you see how nice she is with you."

Florette and Cécile shared a passion for gardening and all her life Florette kept a set of gardening tools Cécile had given her. She also gave Florette an insight into the lives of the very rich: "I was always very open with her, more than with the Baroness Alain because she had her outspoken ways. One day I said to her how can you and your friends spend a fortune on a dress that you wear only once, and you aren't even that clothes-mad. For me it's fine because it's how I earn my living, but it seems a little outlandish. She said, Florette, you don't realize that with the life we lead—the servants, the houses, the upkeep—the money we spend on clothes is just a drop in the bucket.

"I had never thought of that," Florette said.

•

It wasn't his lustrous clientele that made Balenciaga world famous: it was the press, whose task was impeded by Balenciaga's distrust, which Mlle Renée and Véra, her enforcer, made unpleasantly clear. The French fashion press, not in the thrall of department store advertisers and still in the 1950s thinking in terms of readers who sewed or had little dressmakers, was not as urgent about the collections as the Americans and, although respectful, not as keen on Balenciaga. His most eager promoters were those Guelphs and Ghibellines of the fashion press, *Vogue* and *Harper's Bazaar*, always referred to as the *Bazaar*, and in terms of column inches Balenciaga was the chief beneficiary of their rivalry.

The work of this deeply serious man elicited the giddiest prose; the excitement is palpable: "by evening, this pneumatic look becomes almost airborne; taffeta as thin as burned paper," "the drama, the discipline," "beautiful, seductive, full of easy luxury," "the quick tang of prophecy," "the woman who owns a Balenciaga, the woman who has never worn an original—both have been converted to the greatness of The Idea."

Diana Vreeland was not yet a power in the 1950s—Florette barely remembered her—and her eccentricity was not compatible with Balenciaga's, being exuberant while his was deeply inhibited, but she praised him in her memoirs as the greatest dressmaker who ever lived: "One never knew what one was going to see at a Balenciaga opening. One fainted. It was possible to blow up and die." The big players were Bettina Ballard at *Vogue* and Carmel (the accent was on the first syllable) Snow at the *Bazaar*. Ballard had been a friend of Balenciaga since 1937, but the brilliant

Snow was mad for him and praised him not only in her pages but in her annual lectures at the Waldorf-Astoria to the influential New York Fashion Group.

Ballard was a lady, Snow ladylike with her soft Irish accent, blue hair, and great personal chic. She claimed to be the discoverer of Balenciaga, said that he fitted her clothes in his Avenue Marceau apartment and tended to have a proprietary air, stating in her memoirs that she had introduced Givenchy to Balenciaga (the two men were clearly too polite, or prudent, to say they had already met). Snow truly believed that Balenciaga's trademark suit with the loose back, semi-fitted front, and standaway collar had been designed especially for her "since I have no neck." She drank a great many of his—or anyone's—martinis. After a well-oiled lunch she would often doze off during the collection, snapping to, so myth had it, when the best number came past. "It wasn't the best number," Florette said, smiling.

It is striking to read the fashion editors' reports today and notice that almost all the attention was focused on Balenciaga's coats and suits, partly because these are what interested professional buyers, partly because mere words, even when studded with dashes and four dots, could not convey the austere extravagance of his evening wear: "Balenciaga pours deep purple chiffon into a now-billowing, now-undulating flow. Draping sweeps the shoulder and—with the first step—cascades into a floating panel that reveals the knee. The effect: effortless of mood as Venus rising from the sea . . ." Evocative, surely, but what is the *Bazaar* talking about?

Ballard left *Vogue* after she failed to be appointed editor when Edna Woolman Chase, who had been there since

A variation on Balenciaga's trademark supple suit

1895, finally retired in 1951. Snow was deposed at the age of seventy in 1957. By then a new crop of photographers had come along who did more for Balenciaga than words ever could. The *Bazaar*'s Richard Avedon photographed models in Balenciagas but his style was a bit too antic, while *Vogue* found a perfect match in the sensitive stillness of Irving Penn. Penn had come to Paris for the first time in 1950 and in his old age still spoke with wonder of the magical light in his rented studio and of his first photos with his wife and model, Lisa Fonssagrives. If it was only Penn who was able to capture the sculptural quality of Balenciaga's clothes, it took Fonssagrives to dissipate their solemnity: no model has ever been so lovely and amused.

Karl Lagerfeld, then a German teenager, saw his first Balenciaga in a Penn photo of Lisa in the September 1950 *Vogue* (he had never before seen Balenciaga, Penn, or even *Vogue*) and suddenly sensed there could be a life for him in fashion. The overwritten caption meant nothing to him, but the image "was a triumph of real elegance," he later said. "I could feel by instinct that this was the right vision, the vision to follow."

It all should have been wonderful, and it was, except that Penn hated the house of Balenciaga and dealing with "those women in black, my enemies," he told me many years later in New York. If he was going there to buy a dress for an advertising campaign they smothered him in politeness, but to photograph clothes for *Vogue* he had to go to the Avenue George V (other couturiers let the dresses go for photo sessions) and use the back door. "So we wouldn't run into customers," he explained. "Everyone else," he added, "came to *Vogue* with bells on."

Irving Penn's 1950 picture inspired a young Karl Lagerfeld

•

One day, when Carmel Snow was having lunch with Balenciaga at the Grand Véfour, she saw Paulette Goddard and Anita Loos at a nearby table with the aged writer Colette. Knowing how much they admired Balenciaga, she beckoned her two friends over to the table. "When I performed the introductions," she wrote, "without a moment's hesitation, without even glancing at each other, both women curtsied to Balenciaga as Englishwomen curtsey to royalty."

That's the sort of thing that happened to Cristóbal Balenciaga in the 1950s.

The tradesman in him had to be pleased and the artist gratified, although he was incapable of satisfaction, always believing he could do better. The reaction of the man himself remains opaque, one reason being that he was so rarely around. He would prepare the collections in Paris, and then when they were over go to Spain to recuperate and to oversee his Spanish houses. The Spanish collections were labeled Eisa rather than Balenciaga but were identical to the French. "The Spanish *premiers* came to Paris," Florette said, "but they didn't know how to give that *petit chic parisien.* The clothes were less effective and, since the fabric used was Spanish, cheaper." Balenciaga had flats in Barcelona and Madrid and, in Igueldo, in the Basque country near Getaria, a beautiful and simple very Spanish house, with dark furniture smelling of beeswax and his mother's sewing machine displayed as if it were a work by his friend, the sculptor Eduardo Chillida. "Cristóbal and Chillida were Basque, both had that strong and true side," Givenchy says.

In the winter, Balenciaga added ski trips combined with visits to his sinus specialist in Zurich. Apart from what duty required and friendship rewarded, he made no attempt to be part of the Paris social scene. His apartment on the fifth floor of a stolid 1882 building at 28 Avenue Marceau, around the corner from work, had mostly Louis XVI furniture upholstered in dark green, and white curtains. He would have preferred the stronger Régence style but knew it wouldn't go with the building's ornately plastered ceilings.

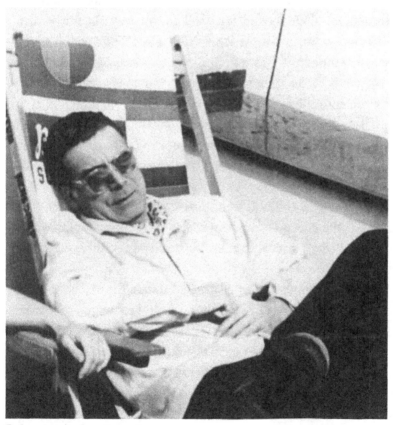

Balenciaga relaxes at winter sports

He met many artists through the printer and gallerist Aimé Maeght but did not collect paintings, although he did have a rather muddy Braque seascape. He preferred antique Spanish silver and old bronze keys—objects that, like Chillida's sculptures and, for that matter, his own work, were textured and tactile.

Although pictured as solitary, he did have friends such as the worldly jeweler Jean ("Johnny") Schlumberger, who sent him Bunny Mellon as a client. "With friends he was very open, very kind," said Schlumberger's companion, Luc Bouchage. "One looked forward to an evening with him." Dinners were in the Avenue Marceau. "The food was always wonderful, French and very good, although there was very little wine served and the glasses were small. People complained."

Balenciaga made Schlumberger copies in blue of the short white smock he always worked in, and he would take Schlumberger's sister, Jacqueline, off to Igueldo and make clothes for her. Always happiest when he was cutting or pinning or sewing, he enjoyed the visits more than she did. "She used to say there were so very few people around, it was a very strict atmosphere, rather lonely at times," Bouchage said.

The invisible waves of creation that Peter Brook spoke of were never still. Balenciaga's sleeves were, of course, endlessly inventive from the start of the decade. There was the melon sleeve of 1950, falling from a dropped shoulder in folds like the skin of a plump shar-pei puppy, the bell sleeve, the tulip, the kimono, and what *Women's Wear Daily* in 1951 hailed as a sleeve "with chicken-leg fullness." The same year *Vogue* cited the Chinese lantern sleeve and the enigma sleeve, wisely perhaps not attempting to describe them though labeling them IMPORTANT. But Balenciaga hated novelty for its own sake, and his line developed consistently and organically.

In the profitably dystopian fashions of our times, it is hard to imagine an approach whose aim, and achievement, was quite simply beauty: a beauty that because it evolved

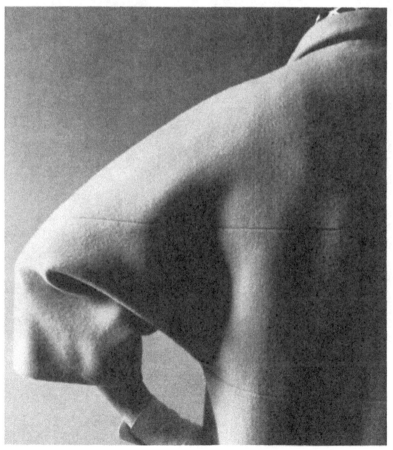

The twin-seamed sleeve

The melon sleeve

The sack dress

The baby doll dress

naturally could endure. The barrel line of 1947, expansive at the waist and gathered at the hem, became the loosely fitted suit (1951) and the classic tunic (1955), which became the sheath, still a basic form today, which then transmuted to the cleverly built sack dress of 1957—infamous when cheaply copied worldwide—and then in 1958 became the lightweight fluted trapezoid called the baby doll.

One might not wish to look like a baby doll, but from its fluting Balenciaga developed the wildly beautiful ruffles that would enhance the drama of his evening wear. And all women benefited—and benefit still—from the principal achievement of his 1950s lines: the elimination of a tight nipped-in waist and the smoother, more yielding silhouette that still obtains today. Balenciaga, Emanuel Ungaro said, is conjugated in the present tense.

He worked closely with his favorite fabric manufacturers, his eye so precise that he never ordered a centimeter too much (if a client's body required even an extra fifty centimeters, the order had to be signed by Balenciaga himself). With Gustav Zumsteg in Switzerland he developed his favorite fabric, gazar, a nubbed silk based on cotton bandages that took Zumsteg three years to perfect and that fell in the deep, rich folds that Balenciaga sought. His tweeds came from England, lightened when American clients complained that they were too warm for central heating, and his prints from Lyons.

One flowered print worn by the hefty and garrulous Margaret Biddle was alone proof of Balenciaga's genius, a friend, Garith Windsor, told me years ago: "She kept talking and talking and out of boredom I began counting the cabbage roses around her waist. When I added them up,

I could hardly believe it." Give me an imperfect body and I will make it perfect, Balenciaga used to say. "A bit pretentious," Florette said, "but true."

His workday began with his Basque secretary, Gérard Chucca, announcing, "Monsieur is here." In the studio Gérard was always at his elbow taking notes, as were Esparza and Gérard's partner, Fernando Martínez, who sketched his ideas (Balenciaga sketched badly). The machine-gun rattle of Balenciaga losing his temper in Spanish was shattering, a favorite epithet being *cursi*, which journalists translated as "vulgar" but which seems to suggest something worse, piss-elegant or downright common.

Odette, Lili's assistant, sometimes found it all too Spanish. The one French habitué of Balenciaga's private domain was the Basque André Courrèges, whom Balenciaga soon encouraged to open his own house, generously giving him backing and clients after asking Courrèges to find a replacement, which took three years. The replacement was Emanuel Ungaro. This did not mean that Balenciaga liked what Courrèges did on his own: some years later, when Nicole Parent was at the movies with another former model, they realized when the lights came up that Balenciaga was seated nearby. "I said to him, And here I am wearing Courrèges. Courrèges, he said, let me see. He looked me over. My God, that is ugly, he said."

Change was in the air, not only with the opening of Courrèges. In 1955 Karl Lagerfeld got his first job, at Balmain. In 1957 Yves Saint Laurent began his short stint as chief designer at Dior. And in 1953 Hubert de Givenchy met Balenciaga at a party given by Condé Nast's Iva S. V. Patchévitch in New York, having tried earlier in Paris and been thrown out by Mlle Renée. Givenchy had just opened his own small house after making accessories for Schiaparelli's boutique. He was twenty-six years old, well-born and poised, immensely tall, and so handsome with his shock of dark hair, blue eyes, and noble nose, said the Balenciaga model Danielle Slavik, that traffic stopped when he crossed the Avenue George V.

After that meeting, Balenciaga invited Givenchy to have lunch at a New York restaurant, L'Aiglon. "I remember that just as I remember everything he said, so great was my affection," Givenchy recalled. "He started to tell me about his life. He said, You know I don't look at fashion magazines much, but I find in your work a freshness and charm. He spoke of an organdy scarf with a lily of the valley motif. That he remembered that touched me.

Balenciaga at a fitting, with Emanuel Ungaro at left

Hubert de Givenchy

"Little by little, from this friendship grew something much bigger." Givenchy respected Balenciaga's honesty, the discretion that people mistook for secretiveness, his naturalness. "He had the simplicity he always kept of a man born poor in a little village. He was perhaps impressed by his clientele but he always remained what he had been, close to his family and to the way he had been raised." He teased Givenchy for being so costively _comme il faut._ "He would say to me, You have an upbringing that says you must be this, you must do that. No, be natural, be simple, be honest, don't make complications."

One Sunday in Spain, Balenciaga took Givenchy to his empty atelier. "There were all those dummies of Spanish women who, like anyone at a certain moment in life, Spanish or not, had bent backs and sagging bosoms. Esparza was there and we passed the pins—they had to be passed in a certain way and we couldn't pass them fast enough—and we could see the woman starting to straighten up. It was wonderful to see little by little, and just with pins, the body rebalance itself. It was plastic surgery to the highest degree."

Givenchy's own technique was not strong, and he told Balenciaga he would like to study incognito in his Barcelona atelier. "He said—he was a man who always spoke the truth—That's useless, don't try for the impossible. You have taste, Hubert, your taste will get you through life. You have _premiers_—he did, by the way, give me two of his—and the ones I gave you will help with your technique. With your taste, you will give them ideas and you will learn from them. It's too late for you to pick up the craft, but watch them and learn."

Which Givenchy did, and one can imagine Balenciaga's pleasure as mentor to this dazzling young man. But in the house of Balenciaga the effects were devastating, and at least four of his associates spoke to me of Givenchy with bitterness. The crisis apparently came when Balenciaga decided to give Givenchy funds to move his couture house to larger premises across the street from Balenciaga on the Avenue George V. One might think that what Balenciaga did with his money was his own business, but there was talk that he had been manipulated by his new friend. Nicolás Bizcarrondo, Balenciaga's cofounder and financial director, advised Balenciaga not to make the gift, with the result that Balenciaga simply threw his old friend and benefactor out. Bizcarrondo, his grand-niece says, never recovered. Asked about the split, Givenchy says he knew nothing about Bizcarrondo, who had already left when he met Balenciaga in 1953. But legal records show that Bizcarrondo went in 1955.

Nicole Parent remembers crying when she bade the Bizcarrondos good-bye, and Jean-Claude Janet said that Balenciaga came over to explain himself—"like one side in a divorcing couple."

Givenchy got his new building, and of the three original partners, d'Attainville, Bizcarrondo, and Balenciaga, only Balenciaga was left to enter the new decade, his last as a designer, on his own.

5

Balenciaga could do as he pleased, and he did. In 1956 he barred the press from his collections until the commercial buyers and clients had seen them. What was viewed as high and mighty behavior was based on Balenciaga's fear of copyists: during the four-week press ban, orders for manufacturers could be made and safely delivered. The move was not entirely reasonable, since buyers were just as larcenous as the press, but buyers bought, while Balenciaga never could see much use in the press. Givenchy joined him in the ban.

The *New York Herald Tribune*'s feisty Eugenia Sheppard, who was once bounced from the house for referring to Balenciaga as the Big Daddy of the Haute Couture, reacted by interviewing buyers in the Ritz bar after they had seen the show. "Well, it was gay at the Ritz and don't think black marketing reporting can't be fun," she wrote on August 1, 1957.

More significantly, the ban meant that *Vogue* and *Harper's Bazaar* had to cover the collections twice, the first time writing on the other designers, the second—a month later—on the two rebels. Givenchy benefited from being seen alone with the couture's top name, and since fashion editors had to pad out the first article, they allowed more space for younger designers such as Yves Saint Laurent, giving them a boost that otherwise might have been seasons in coming.

For the moment, Balenciaga had no serious competitors. John Fairchild, who had come to Paris in 1955 to lighten up his family's trade journal, *Women's Wear Daily*, with fashion gossip, made a habit of stalking him, and in 1962, after tracking Balenciaga for two years, he published seven photographs—"the first pictures in ten years by any publication anywhere in the world"—of Balenciaga with Esparza in Madrid's flea market. "Balenciaga is still king," the text read. "Where he steps, the rest of fashion follows." The same year, even *France-Soir* snapped him on the Avenue George V wearing his white work smock. "This isn't a barber," explained the caption. "This is Balenciaga, the mystery man."

He was producing more accessories, not only as a profitable sideline but in order to give a total look. His gloves, Givenchy says, were better than those from Hermès, and Florette showed me a truly wonderful pair of hers: the softest suede, called peach skin, or *peau de pêche*, in a rich deep blue—total luxury with an easy air because the fingertips were slightly blunted and the cuffs were loose, rather like gardening gloves. Balenciaga showed the first patterned tights, the orthopedic-looking laced shoes and high boots still worn today, and, because he thought no outfit complete without a hat, the pillbox that Givenchy used so effectively on Audrey Hepburn and Jacqueline Kennedy Onassis.

His colors became more and more brilliant. "You've

Daytime wool ensemble with straw hat, 1961

The grand gesture as summarized by Penn

"Balenciaga is still king"

never seen such colors," Diana Vreeland wrote, "you've never seen such violets! My God, pink violets, blue violets!" In 1965, the year of Saint Laurent's primary-colored Mondrian line, Balenciaga showed unimagined combinations of bottle green and ginger, camel beige with charcoal gray, black with brown. At one Balenciaga show, Vreeland says, "Audrey Hepburn turned to me and asked why I wasn't frothing at the mouth at what I was seeing . . . Across the way, Gloria Guinness was sliding out of her chair onto the floor. Everyone was going up in foam and thunder. We didn't know what we were doing, it was so glorious."

As usual, Balenciaga was obsessively perfecting his line rather than changing it with each season. The physical wear and tear was great—after a full day of 150 fittings he would sometimes go back to his studio and work into the night—and was only bearable because he spent as much time as he could in Spain, supervising the Madrid and Barcelona houses and, above all, recovering in Igueldo, where his sister Agustina acted as housekeeper until her death in 1966. Givenchy remembers going with him to the local market to watch him happily debate in Basque with the fishmongers. "Everyone knew him and called him Cristóbal. He would look under the gills and say no, no, that's not fresh, it wasn't caught last night." One of the bawling fishwives, Balenciaga told Givenchy with his charming smile, was a big client at his Barcelona branch.

In Paris he walked daily up the Avenue Marceau to his parish church, Saint Pierre de Chaillot (Balenciaga made the cassock for its priest, Father Pieplu, as he had for his priests in Spain). Sometimes he would call Givenchy at five o'clock, telling him to stop work and come along. "I am a

Protestant but I felt honored to go with him," Givenchy said. As Balenciaga's last living intimate he is our closest connection to him, eager to equate Balenciaga's *justesse* of line with his honesty: "For me he was *un homme parfait*, he had an integrity such as I have never seen."

But even Givenchy is sometimes troubled by this luminous man's darker shadings. He still shudders when he speaks of two of Balenciaga's terrible rages, one as a mourner at the funeral of a friend who he felt had cheated him, when Balenciaga suddenly began to shout, and in the Madrid workroom when he let loose at a seamstress who had forgotten to hang her measuring tape around her neck: "She wasn't young and she wept. He wouldn't let up."

Givenchy is most vivid when he speaks of how the truth of the man was expressed in the smallest details. "I saw the most beautiful breakfast tray in my life in his house. The tray was simple, with a linen mat of the most extraordinary quality, a bit rough, and a china cup of beautiful volume. The butter dish was eighteenth-century glass, the milk pitcher was Spanish, more sturdy than refined. Everything was true, was honest, was solid. He never chose anything chi-chi. Everything had a huge force, a personality that was reflected in everything, because even the linen had a rough side. It wasn't Porthault, it was Balenciaga."

As keeper of the flame, Givenchy doesn't like Balenciaga to be viewed as dour or opaque and insists on his love of laughter and his marvelous smile. He enjoyed dishing with Marie-Louise Bousquet and Mitza Bricard, Givenchy says, and he didn't always dress in black. "He liked good food and gave amusing dinners. Greta Garbo came, and once I saw Luis Mariano there, all in white." Luis Mariano

The essence of Balenciaga

was the star of popular operettas at the Châtelet, a Liberace figure with capped white teeth and a slick black hairpiece. Givenchy raised his eyebrows, to which Balenciaga replied, "But he is charming, very religious, and very correct. And he is Basque."

Except for rare obligatory events, Balenciaga was in no way part of the Paris scene and had no wish to be. In her 1956 book *Paris à la Mode*, Célia Bertin found the clothes of "Christobal" [*sic*] Balenciaga difficult and austere: "The style of the Spanish couturier is that of a closed universe, without apparent connection with everyday life, without even much regard for Parisian forms and faces."

Many of his clients were French because a well-dressed woman *had* to have Balenciagas, but his often-severe lines were at odds with the Parisian love of decorative dresses made to flatter and charm. He was more an international than a French couturier, and the French couture, which had welcomed such foreigners as Schiaparelli and Molyneux before the war, was now more chauvinistic, facing competition from Italy and the United States. Spain, fashionable in France from the days of Empress Eugénie through Salvador Dalí, was seen in the dwindling Franco days of the 1960s as a poor and backward country, a cheap supplier of domestic help and not a source of the new.

At least two French fashion chroniclers cruelly mocked Balenciaga's pronunciation of the word *tissu* as *tissou*. His Spanish accent may be one reason people always said he spoke very softly. Paris society is a self-regarding minefield through which Dior and Balmain knew how to undulate. Balenciaga never made a faux pas because he never made a *pas* at all.

Balenciaga (left) fits Mme Zumsteg at La Reynerie

The women he really liked to dress, French or not, were oddly enough small, plump, and middle-aged—Mme Bizcarrando, Mme Maeght, Mme Kandinsky, the widow of the painter, Mme Zumsteg, and Janine Janet, his window dresser. They were part of his experiments in sculpting form: "Monsieur likes a bit of belly" was the saying in the house.

Their roly-poly bodies told him how to confer, or to enhance, beauty. From such unlikely shapes, and from the precision he had already reached in his coats and suits, Balenciaga invented for his lissome swans evening wear that was abundant but cut by a geometer's hand: the most spectacular evening clothes ever seen, said *Vogue*, meant

There was vinelike green embroidery traced on a heavy satin dress with a scattering of brilliant orange flowers, there were stoles, floor-length or three-pointed, a white velvet floor-length cape based on a fisherman's net. Ruffles, which he liked, burst with power and never simpered; the flare on a long skirt could have been chamfered rather than cut by scissors, but was supple, not stiff. No detail, even the tiniest flower, was merely decorative: the dresses were showpieces of authenticity. No other designer could be so heartbreakingly simple, or so irrevocably complex.

The short front and trailing back, a Balenciaga favorite

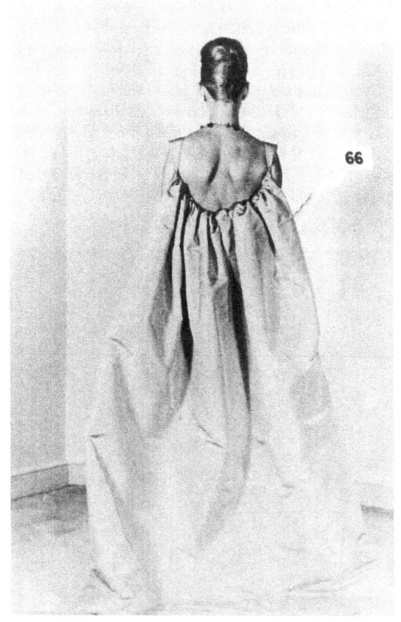

66

A typical Balenciaga train

The fashion writer's killer words, "wearable" and "pretty," were never applied to Balenciaga's clothes. Not only did the evening clothes demand assurance and a sense of style but they could also be damnably hard to put on. "Balenciaga is such a trying man," the Duchess of Windsor complained, "he makes one pull everything over the head. It is ruinous to the hair." Florette, when we looked together at the color plates in Marie-Andrée Jouve's book on Balenciaga, wondered how her clients actually managed to wear what she had sold them. He often used a short front hemline that flowed to floor length at the rear—lovely, but how to get into a taxi? How did the woman in the balloon dress, which was shaped like one, sit down? How did the wearer of a trumpet-shaped long sleeve avoid dipping it into her dinner?

Such questions were not posed by the women who could carry such clothes, and pay for them. Mona Bismarck took eighty-eight numbers in 1963, fairly typical except for the year when many of her clothes were in a train wreck and she ordered one hundred fifty Balenciagas all at once. His biggest client of all was Mrs. Paul Mellon, who, like Mona, had him make her gardening clothes, though she didn't have the legs for Mona's shorts: "Being a working gardener," she wrote, "I had big cotton or linen blouses with plain blue denim skirts, each slit to the knees."

One client who may have supplied comic relief was Claudia Heard de Osborne, a good-looking Texas oil heiress who had married into the Spanish sherry-producing Osborne family and traveled between the Ritz in Paris and the Ritz in Madrid, where she kept several rooms just for her clothes. Her enthusiasm was as exuberant as her orders, but her taste was curious. For a ball, Balenciaga designed especially for her a black velvet long gown with a bustle to which were affixed many tiny ermine tails. It is arguably the ugliest dress he ever made. She regarded herself as an intimate: she condoled with Balenciaga on the death of both his sister, Agustina, and his Yorkshire terrier, Plume; she thrillingly submitted to having her Balenciaga jacket ripped apart because of the sleeve after they had had lunch together; she wept with him after he closed. Unhappy with Spain's post-Franco democratic government, in 1975 she consigned three hundred of her Balenciagas to the University of North Texas, noting that in parting with them she had stained them with her tears.

Balenciaga's favorite, and one of his closest friends, was Sonsoles, Marquesa de Llanzol, a client since the 1940s and a confidante whom he addressed in the familiar *tú*. Florette, like his other French employees, thought that the marquesa, being Spanish, was distinguished but lacked style until she dressed at the Paris, as well as the Madrid, house, but her daughter, Sonsoles Díez de Rivera, says the tall, fair marquesa was considered the most elegant woman in Madrid. Sonsolita, as she was called, knew Balenciaga from the age of seven. "He was like an uncle," she said. "I never realized he was secretive or timid or whatever, he was always enormously nice to me. He and my mother were very close. She was a very witty woman, very intelligent and cultivated, and he always had a lovely time with her. So I always saw him relaxed, not stiff. It was a great privilege, which I didn't realize until much later."

Sonsolita first went to Paris at the age of fifteen, driving through the Loire Valley with her mother, followed by

The balloon dress

Balenciaga and his favorite client and friend, the Marquesa de Llanzol

Balenciaga in a car with Esparza and his chauffeur. "Finally we got to Paris and we stayed in his apartment. My mother then was very young, she must have been thirty-six or something like that, and my father didn't come along, so she found herself very free and wanted to go out every night, which Balenciaga found very funny. So we always went out, the four of us, to all sorts of nightclubs and the Lido, that sort of thing. After that I'd be tired because I was only fifteen and my mother didn't want to go to bed, she wanted to go to the Quartier Latin and Les Halles for onion soup. So they went for their onion soup while I slept on Esparza's shoulder, and there they were chatting along and having great fun, both of them."

Balenciaga made young Sonsoles's first communion dress and, in 1957, her wedding gown. He did not ask her

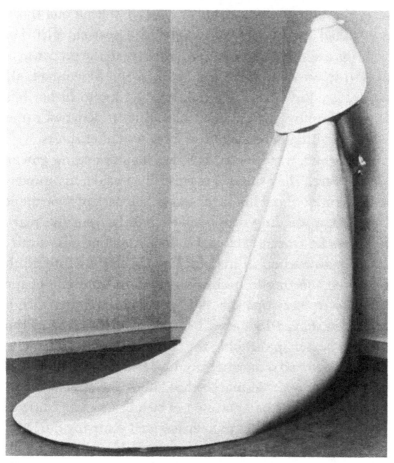

Wedding gown with "coal-scuttle" headdress, 1967

what she wanted. "I was only eighteen and no one those days asked the opinion of an eighteen-year-old girl. He said, You are very dark, like the Madonna in the processions in Seville, so we'll make a gown like the Madonna's, all embroidered in silver." He didn't have time to fit her but made a dummy and cut the toiles himself. Esparza came to the wedding; Balenciaga was away at winter sports.

The gown was superb, as Balenciaga's wedding gowns always were. They suited his sense of occasion, his stupendous technique, and his emphasis on the back of a garment (after all, a wedding dress is seen mostly from the rear). His dress for Queen Fabiola, Givenchy told me, was a miracle of construction in his placing of a heavy white mink border on the fragile neckline and train. And one of his last masterpieces was the 1967 gazar bridal gown with a headdress shaped like a coal scuttle over the nape of the neck, its oval shape echoing the curve of the train. Danielle Slavik, blond and somewhat shy, modeled the dress and says it was easy to wear, despite the headdress, and often ordered.

Danielle, who had planned to be a beautician, came to Balenciaga in 1964 just to keep a friend company during a model call. "I had colored my hair myself and I had a spot on my dress so I put it on backwards. I was sitting with a bunch of girls in the grand salon when I heard myself called by Mademoiselle Renée, and suddenly in the salon there was Monsieur Balenciaga and Monsieur Esparza and they asked me to walk. I couldn't raise my head, I was so *mal à l'aise.* Then Mademoiselle Renée put me in a suit, Monsieur Balenciaga went back into his studio, and I was asked when I could start."

First, Balenciaga had to show her the Balenciaga walk.

Queen Fabiola's mink-trimmed wedding gown: "a miracle of construction," according to Givenchy

"One day he took me by the arm and walked next to me to show me the rhythm. He would say, Boom, boom, boom, slow but not too slow and look straight ahead." Although he could explode during fittings that might last into the night (when they did, he would send Danielle home in a taxi or his car), he was unfailingly paternal to his models.

"I always thought my thighs were a bit heavy. One day I was dizzy during a fitting and Monsieur Balenciaga asked me what was wrong. I explained that I was on a diet and he said, Danielle, it's not your job to slim, it's my job to dress you so it can't be seen. Imagine! And he had the restaurant at the corner, the Relais de l'Alma, send up a steak and French fries. He and Monsieur Esparza stood over me until I ate it all."

His benevolence did not temper his terrifying vigilance. When a young assistant named Claudia passed by laden with ten hats, Balenciaga stopped her with the words "You look like you're carrying a load of melons," although she was Mlle Renée's niece. Fittings were torture for the *premiers d'atelier*, Danielle says. "He would start off smiling and lose his temper within five minutes. It would go on until the eve of the collection. The *premiers* would think a dress was finished and then Monsieur Balenciaga would ask to see it again and it was *la catastrophe*. The *premiers* always hoped he wouldn't notice them."

He even surveyed photographers. Danielle, while pretty, was not photogenic, but for a while Balenciaga had a rule that photographers had to use his house models, with the result that the heads were cut off in many printed pictures. He threw Twiggy out when she came with a photographer, insisting that one of his girls be used instead.

A fitting on Danielle Slavik

In their *cabines* the eight models crocheted or told each other's fortunes. When summoned to Balenciaga's studio for a fitting, they put on a lightweight black satin underdress, or *fond de robe*, embroidered with their names, worn so that pins would not catch in their undergarments. "I think Monsieur Balenciaga also had us wear them for reasons of modesty," Danielle said. The girls didn't necessarily get along, but Danielle's biggest problems came from, of all people, Florette.

"She was jealous because she wanted Anita Delion, her niece, to get my job. She would say things like I don't know why he hired you, and when a private client came she would ask for another model to show my clothes."

They became friends later but the beginning was rough. "I was so frightened at my first collection," Danielle said, "that my fingers couldn't button the coat I was showing. Some of the vendeuses helped me, but not Florette."

Florette's success didn't make her popular in the house, and she could be short-tempered given how sore her feet were despite the four pairs of Mancini pumps that she wore out each year. Her voice had become more worldly in her fifties, her manner more assured. She was the only vendeuse who needed two assistants (and sometimes three), whom she paid from her own pocket—another niece, also named Anita, and Betsy, a broken-down marquise *qui avait eu des malheurs*. Betsy was sweet but fairly useless, though Florette said she was good at handling the ateliers. Florette was perhaps rather pleased to have a marquise in her employ.

Payot, semi-retired, loyally prepared dinner and soothed

her nerves at the end of the day, although he didn't much like it when people called him M. Florette. "What was exceptional about them was their mutual admiration. Payot was always praising her, saying she was the highest paid vendeuse in Paris, and Florette admired his culture," says Benoît Gaubert, son of the Chelots' oldest friends. The Gauberts were prosperous shopkeepers with two stationery stores in central Paris. Georges Clemenceau was a client and Colette ordered her famous blue writing paper from the Papeterie Gaubert.

In the summers the Gauberts would rent a house near the Chelots' *maison du bonheur* in Normandy. When in town they dined together (Benoît tasted his first foie gras at the Chelots'), and on Saturday afternoons they boated, paddling up the Seine from Paris and taking the train back. Benoît was uneasy with Florette because, like many childless women, she fussed over him too much. His mother felt intimidated, too, and never went to a Balenciaga show (that wasn't her world, Benoît says). Although embarrassed when, in her new fancy voice, Florette complimented him on his shapely legs, M. Gaubert had the greatest respect for her. "My father considered her an exceptional woman. He would say, She is always at ease, always at home everywhere. That was what he most admired."

Florette was indeed at ease and made others feel the same, to the point where the clients of other vendeuses felt they could ask her advice. "Dear Florette," the socialite Mrs. Gilbert ("Kitty") Miller wrote to her from New York. "Would you be very kind and write me a little letter with the numbers of the models you think I would like. I don't wish to hurt Lily's feelings and let her think I have consulted with you, but I think you have wonderful taste and you know which dresses are good for me."

Her order book bulged, her figure was svelte in her black Balenciaga, her hair tight in its tidy chignon. She sat at her vendeuse's desk radiating confidence and good humor. That was the Florette I met in the early 1960s, when I went to the house of Balenciaga for the first time.

I was more curious than scared. The ground floor boutique was quiet, the ride to the third floor in the cordovan-leather-lined elevator smooth. The first sight of Véra, scowling in greeting, caused me a qualm or two; so

Balenciaga's top vendeuse goes to work

did walking between two rows of vendeuses gazing up from their desks in bored contempt. I was wearing a cotton shirtwaist dress. My friend George carried a pot of home-made jam. We reached Florette's desk, third on the left, and she looked up and smiled.

George was young and English, a remittance man paid a tiny monthly allowance to stay away from the family bank in Hong Kong. We were each living in crummy hotel rooms and we were both short of cash and idle, I because I was unsuccessfully job hunting, George because he had no intention of dulling his existence with work. He spoke half a dozen languages, knew everyone, and cooked lunch on his hot plate for worldly women whom he charmed and amused. It was after one of those luncheons that he tele-phoned me and said we were off to take some jam to his new friend, Florette.

We had already been to all the collections, so I was fa-miliar with the lily of the valley scent of Dior and wifely glamour at Balmain. In those days the couture houses showed their collections afternoons at three o'clock for a month or so after the openings, and anyone with the time—of which we had plenty—could drop by after the buyers and big spenders had gone. (This was long before the collections became one-shot musical extravaganzas in eccentric venues—Prada at the Communist Party head-quarters, Lagerfeld filling the huge dome of the Grand Palais with dry ice, macabre McQueen recalling the execu-tion of Marie-Antoinette at the Conciergerie.) Balenciaga was the grandest to watch, sublimely out of reach.

I yearned but I knew nothing, having been brought up in New York to think that fashion was for other people. As a teenager I wore Tangee lipstick and wished it were Fire and Ice, I had crinolines and Capezios and wanted them to be sheaths and spike heels. Our parents thought we should look like Doris Day, we would have preferred Lauren Bacall (both of them, although so different, born in 1924). It was still a time of Junior Miss departments whose style was more virginal than young. We wore panty girdles and Peter Pan collars, staid and safely sexless. The whole point, I think, was to keep us from being what we most wanted to be: grown-up. Our mentors were not *Harper's* or *Vogue* but our mothers, not Why Don't You? but don't you dare.

By the time I was in college, my parents took me to buy a short evening dress from the very fashionable Simonetta in Rome. I was so dazzled at having the glamorous raven-haired designer kneel at my feet to adjust the hem that I didn't really pay attention to the dress. It was strapless and peach-colored with a bouffant skirt, every centimeter covered in tiny peach bows. Leave it to my mother to find it, but what was it doing in that worldly maison de couture to begin with? I wore it only once, to a party in Monte Carlo where it was totally out of place and where a guest threw up over it in the ladies' room.

While George chatted wittily to Florette I hung back, wide-eyed. Wide-eyed was not what Balenciaga customers were, and later she told me that this had touched her. I was about the same height as the best house model, Taiga, and I suppose my shyness could have passed for dignity. At any rate, first thing I knew, Florette was rummaging around a closet filled with past seasons' Taigas, the wonderful tailor

Salvador had been summoned, and I was out of my shirt-waist and into a blue light wool Balenciaga suit. Florette sold it—gave it to me, really—for a price that was absurdly low. Mlle Renée would not have been pleased.

I remember how easy and right that suit felt, as nothing had before, and how it gave me confidence when finally I found a job at the Paris *Herald Tribune* at $60 a week. I began on the women's page, not covering fashion, which I never have done, but providing such features as I could find.

Since I was fascinated by fashion history as a reflection of its times, I sought out retired designers to interview. The first was Schiaparelli, more interested during the sixties in trying her hand at painting than in the current fashion scene: "Fashion collections bore me," she said. The sole designer who interested her was Balenciaga because "he is the only one who dares do what he likes." The second interview was with Madeleine Vionnet.

She lived in a town house at 3 bis Square Antoine Arnauld in the Sixteenth Arrondissement of Paris. It had a rather bulbous bourgeois façade with a stunning Art Deco interior of museum quality—sleek and cool, with lacquer surfaces and Jean-Michel Frank furniture. The walls of the salon were lined in parchment and on one of them hung a portrait—by the 1920s master of lacquer Jean Dunand—of the plump Vionnet in her heyday looking like a stiff society hostess. "I hate it, it was never me," she remarked. It certainly showed none of the liveliness of eye or the quickness of mind that her much slimmer self retained in her late eighties. Balenciaga's bright red skirt and vest reinforced her vividness in a rather beige décor, as he had surely intended. She had just returned from a visit to Natalie Clifford

Barney and on the way there saw her first miniskirt: "It is horrible to play with proportions that way. I was the first to lower waistlines to suit my own proportions. Now when I see women in tops that are longer than their skirts I am ashamed to think it may be my fault."

"Do you write about couture?" she asked me, and I said no, figuring that would be the end of the interview. "That's good," she said, "because couture is finished." It was not only a lack of talent but changing lifestyles: the growth of air travel and lightweight suitcases, she predicted, would be a final blow.

Having closed her own house some twenty-five years earlier, Vionnet had passed on to other interests. In her sixties she taught herself the piano and in her eighties learned to read Russian. "No," she said, "I can't speak it but I can read it and translate it, which isn't bad." A book in Russian lay nearby, along with Edgar Wallace in English, some thrillers, and a biography of Sir Alexander Fleming, the discoverer of penicillin. "When I created all day, morning to night, I couldn't use my energy on reading. Now I am reading, starting everything all over again."

She was great fun to talk to once we had got past couture, given to statements that I still remember, such as "Almost always, when you see a picture called *Mother of the Painter*, it's good." She died after Balenciaga, in her ninety-ninth year. When her goddaughter asked if she looked forward to reaching one hundred, she replied, "Not at all, it simply isn't done."

With such encounters I was learning a lot. It seemed to me that while an American childhood teaches us to be good and to try to be better, the French show us how to be more attractive. The difference isn't as frivolous as it sounds since it encompasses a more precise use of language, a sharpening of the senses, in all a critical eye open to what Henry James called "a completeness of form" that he found only in France. I struggled then, and struggle still today, to reach this mysterious balance between measure and indulgence of which I was not even aware until, about as incomplete as a young American can be, I found myself in Florette's hands.

It was all very casual: I would drop in, and if she had the time she would forage for leftovers, sometimes from several seasons past. They weren't trailing ballgowns or matadors' jackets, which I couldn't have afforded, even at Florette's prices, and anyway I had no place to wear them. Mostly they were sleeveless wool dresses, but there was a beautiful black silk crepe for evening, the collarless gray tweed coat, and even a brown suede suit, as well as a couple of mistakes, like the rather elderly pink crepe dress with its pink lace coat for $150 noted in Florette's order book for 22 June 1966. (Most of my purchases were not listed in her book since they were near giveaways.)

I could go to 10 Avenue George V wearing the most uneventful outfit and emerge with the certainty that to the knowing, or even to the ignorant, eye I was well dressed. A Balenciaga could be outlandishly showy or, like mine, almost plain. What they all had, uniquely, was poise—a savant equilibrium that was quiet even at its most extravagant—and this poise was passed on to the wearer. It was my blue light wool Balenciaga suit that enabled me to take out a notepad and quiz Eleanor Roosevelt at the Hotel de Crillon as if I were (almost) entitled to.

Whether you were Mrs. Mellon or a motor tycoon's plump wife or a tyro journalist going to interviews with trembling knees, you knew that despite your imperfections you were, thanks to him, perfect. I remember how easy to wear and *right* my clothes felt.

But if much was conferred by a Balenciaga, much was also exacted: a bearing that excluded slouching, stains, or untoward behavior. For that there was the King's Road and Carnaby Street and all the fun and inconsequence that life suddenly had to offer.

6

Across the Channel, they were having a ball. Mary Quant, the putative inventor of the miniskirt, had opened Bazaar, her King's Road boutique, in 1955, and by 1967 there were more than two thousand small fashion shops in London describing themselves as boutiques. France was way behind. The word boutique may be French but the idea of helter-skelter cheap fashion in kooky little shops was not. Prime Minister Harold Macmillan had presaged the youthquake in all its delicious permissiveness when he told the British people, "You never had it so good." In the suffocating rectitude of General de Gaulle's presidency, such an idea, and such grammar, were unthinkable.

In 1964 a Frenchwoman named Geneviève Antoine Dariaux published a book called *Elegance*, an immensely detailed guide to wearing the right thing, from gloves to pet dogs, but it was already outdated because women now wanted to do the wrong thing. In France, pert little women had practiced their facial expressions—the sidelong glance, the adorable moue, the fetching tilt of the head—until they became second nature. (France, it may be said, is the country of second nature.) Suddenly they had to learn to add spontaneity to their wiles, and to grow longer legs. They began the sorrowful search for youth.

Brigitte Bardot had already announced in 1959 that haute couture was for grandmas, but she was shocking by habit and an example to no one. Couture's solemnity was now relieved by such designers as Emanuel Ungaro, who refused to show evening clothes in his first collection in 1965 because "I am a man of this age and I will design for women of this age," and by André Courrèges, who seated clients on stools instead of little gold chairs and had models in his signature white space-age miniskirts dance out to pop tunes. Balenciaga had helped Courrèges from the start and had sent him three clients, including Florette's Begum Aga Khan, a majestic figure with, says Coqueline Courrèges, thighs like bayonne hams. The Begum was pleased with her Courrèges coat; another Florette client, Cécile de Rothschild, was so offended when Courrèges opened one of his white cube stores opposite her mansion on the Faubourg St. Honoré that she tried to have it shut down.

Balenciaga reigned, although veneration replaced excitement and the word great was diminished by its new modifier, "still." His apartness was seen as Olympian: "Why should he bother dressing the world at this point?" asked *Women's Wear Daily* in 1965. "Vicariously, he does dress a lot of the world when you see how his ideas filter down." The same year, *WWD* published photos snatched of Balenciaga going to work—no fewer than eleven nearly identical pictures of a dapper man in a tilted soft black hat and "legendary one-button overcoat," with a small map inserted to show his two-block itinerary between home and work. The word youthful began to appear in journalists' reviews

Women's Wear Daily still stalking Balenciaga in 1965

of Balenciaga, but youthful is not the same as young. Over in swinging London, sassy *Queen* magazine published black-bordered pages in 1964 proclaiming that Balenciaga—and haute couture in general—was dead.

For a few years the old and the new coexisted pleasurably, the new throwaway culture inspiring Cecil Beaton to praise new objects in cheap plastic: "Even the tray you put your drinks on. It becomes a pleasure just to be sitting with four or five people because it all looks so delectable. It takes the place of going to galas and balls," he told me in a 1967 interview on his way to a ball. But it was all changing irrevocably and in every way. The photographer David Bailey says that haute couture as a driving force was dying at just about the time that fast motorized cameras came in: "The dress was a stately sculptured thing before."

Looking at the Metropolitan Museum's 1973 Balenciaga retrospective, Kennedy Fraser wrote that the exhibition was

> a forceful reminder of the speed with which fashion has moved since Balenciaga's reign . . . By the end of the sixties, youth dominated fashion and democracy had come to it, with its attendant choice or confusion, depending on your point of view. Balenciaga's designs are those of an authority, aimed at mature women with a distinct position in the world . . . It is not that the Balenciaga clothes could never be worn by young women, but, rather, that they could be worn with great distinction by those who were no longer young.

Young women were going elsewhere. The Baroness Alain de Rothschild still came to Avenue George V, but her daughter, Béatrice, wasn't interested; the Countess du Boisrouvray continued to sing "Frou-Frou" with Florette, but Albina, her daughter, became a journalist and film producer with no time for fittings. Audrey Hepburn greatly admired Balenciaga and he adored her, even offering to lend her his flat to escape paparazzi, but it would have been unthinkable for her fawnlike body to be dressed by him rather than in Givenchy's slim and cool designs. Already, a decade earlier, Natasha Parry, who, with her husband, Peter Brook, had delighted in Balenciaga's hospitality, never coveted his clothes: "They were so grown-up," she says. When Balenciaga, seeing the writing on the wall, unwisely included short shorts in his last collection, Claudia Heard de Osborne, who might have known better given her age, put in an order. Danielle, the model, told me that she would not have been caught dead in them, even at Cannes.

And I, probably the only Balenciaga client who was there to economize, thanks to Florette's bounty, sometimes had the disloyal desire to go elsewhere, specifically to the new Saint Laurent Rive Gauche.

Saint Laurent's first Rive Gauche boutique opened on September 26, 1966, on the rue de Tournon, in the Sixth Arrondissement of Paris, with Catherine Deneuve as its godmother. Other haute couture designers had boutiques selling separates and accessories, but Saint Laurent was the first to create a complete second line, less expensive but equally chic—*le smoking*, which he had introduced in his latest couture collection, was among the Rive Gauche's first top sellers. Other boutiques offered clothes that were amusing but ill-made (one didn't have to go to design school to cut a miniskirt); Saint Laurent, with his haute couture training and his background as Christian Dior's successor after the designer's death, invented classy French ready-to-wear. It wasn't a question of spinning off more profit, he explained: ready-to-wear was right for the times, for the giddy costume party that was the sixties.

He was the first modern celebrity designer in that he was marketed as much for his persona as his work. Everyone knew that he always named his dogs Moujik, that he used the pseudonym M. Swann when checking into hotels, and that he partied wildly at Régine's; and everyone had seen Jeanloup Sieff's photograph of him in the nude to advertise his men's cologne. In full public view the once beautiful young man disintegrated into a wobbly wraith, fueled by drugs and drink so that he could design two couture collections and two ready-to-wear collections every year. Until, in 2002, he no longer could.

Since each line had to be different from its predecessor, he was a scavenger, a magpie of marketable ideas and the inventor of the quotation-crammed retro look. In hectic profusion he showed clothes influenced by Piet Mondrian, czarist Russia, Morocco, Japan, Spain, Ludwig of Bavaria, Marlon Brando. Tuxedos, pea jackets, safari jackets dictated a new view of femininity; the fact that the safari jacket was inspired by the Afrika Korps of World War II and that he was roundly criticized for a collection based on the German Occupation didn't seem to matter, because questions of taste were considered square. (New York fashion editors, after all, were gushing repellently over "poor-boy sweaters" and "fun furs.") "He understood his times very well, and didn't like them," his partner and Svengali Pierre Bergé has said. His clothes were beautiful and skin-deep.

Saint Laurent mentioned Balenciaga's technique respectfully but found him "insufficiently influenced by life," and Bergé claimed to have dined with Balenciaga at the modish Francine Weisweiller's. Not so, says Givenchy, adding rather tantalizingly, "Cristóbal did make remarks about other designers, but I wouldn't repeat them out of respect for his discretion."

The student uprising in Paris in May 1968, always referred to as *les événements*, or "the events," gave Saint

Laurent a delightful frisson and Balenciaga a scare. "Today, real fashion comes from the young people at the barricades," proclaimed Saint Laurent, omitting to add that he was on holiday in Marrakesh at the time. Balenciaga was in Spain and, like his clients, viewed the photographs of burning cars as the end of the world. It wasn't: the revolution ended as soon as the government took gas off the ration and everyone went off for the long Whitsun weekend during which seventy people were killed in road accidents while, by official count, only one had died during the events. But it was the end of the house of Balenciaga.

He knew that fashion is doomed to be ephemeral, that even the greatest is not, after a while, the most desirable, but he must have had a wish for at least a proper record of his existence because in 1962 he had the photographer Tom Kublin start making films for his own archive of his collections—just a model or two parading through the empty salon. Words never measured up to Balenciaga's work, great magazine photographs were better, but only these modest, badly lighted films (scraps of which are available on YouTube) show how the body moved in a Balenciaga, how it was skimmed, but never straitened, by the clothes.

It is usually claimed that Balenciaga was done in by ready-to-wear, which is and isn't true. Already in the 1950s he had agreed to look at a New York manufacturer's setup, rejecting it not because of the principle but because the quality was poor, and it is said that in Paris in the sixties he occasionally bought other designers' ready-mades to study the technique. He did, after all, know ready-to-wear quite well, having made it in Spain before he even came to France, but he didn't want to water down his skills for something his clientele did not seek. He told Givenchy that although he would have given ready-to-wear a try had he been younger, it was not something to take up toward the end of one's career. He did, in fact, do it once, and with great success: in 1968, aged seventy-three, he designed uniforms for Air France stewardesses, which stayed in production for ten years, until 1978. They had such typical Balenciaga features as knee-high boots and a half-belt on the coat, and although made for the most part from an

Air France uniform

A PROPOS

ON en a beaucoup parlé, on en parle encore beaucoup. Quoi de plus normal ! Les hôtesses de l'air sillonnent la terre ; véritables ambassadrices de la mode française, grâce à elles, le nom du couturier qui a créé leur uniforme est connu jusqu'au bout du monde.

Depuis 1962, c'était la griffe prestigieuse de Christian Dior qui assurait l'élégance des uniformes portés par les hôtesses d'Air France sous tous les ciels du monde. Mais la mode évolue, il fallait changer.

Pour son adieu à la haute couture, en ultime message, le grand couturier Balenciaga s'est vu confier la mission de créer les uniformes qui, dès juin 1969, modifieront la silhouette de nos hôtesses navigantes !

Sa naissance...

Un beau jour d'octobre 1967, on décidait de se livrer à une enquête auprès des hôtesses disponibles à Orly à ce moment-là... Comment concevaient-elles un nouvel uniforme ? On conclut que, le plus souvent, elles souhaitaient lui conserver un caractère classique ; elles le voulaient confortable – surtout pas d'épaisseur qui engonce – élégant, mais pratique et naturellement très féminin.

Balenciaga, avec la rigueur qui le caractérise, demandait alors à étudier les mouvements les plus souvent pratiqués au cours d'un vol. On lui envoya des « commandos » d'hôtesses choisies pour leur type et leur gabarit différents. Il les fit évoluer, les examina avec soin, et en tira de multiples enseignements. Ainsi les poches plaquées sur le haut des manches de la veste d'hiver sont destinées à rétrécir le buste que les poches de poitrine seules auraient pu élargir. Il alla même jusqu'à vérifier sur des uniformes usagés, qu'il se fit apporter, les divers points d'usure.

Sa carte d'identité...

Pour l'hiver, le tailleur bleu marine est en serge pure laine de Marcel Blanc. Jupe droite légèrement évasée qui n'entrave

artificial fabric, Terylene, they were smart and, but for one detail, perfect: despite tryouts on his models, the armholes were, for the first time in Balenciaga's long struggles with *la manga*, not right, too tight for stowing baggage overhead.

Balenciaga belonged to the ocean liner era, although since 1957 more people had been crossing the Atlantic by airplane and steamer trunks were gone from the corridors of the Ritz. Retirement had been in the air for a while,

D'UN UNIFORME

pas la marche, veste près du corps à encolure ronde dégagée pour laisser passer le col du chemisier, en twill de tergal blanc, quatre poches, deux de poitrine, deux sur les manches, fermées par de gros boutons ronds.

Le manteau 7/8 bleu marine également est en très beau shetland. C'est l'élégant et classique manteau Balenciaga. Pas de col, et des emmanchures basses.

Pour l'été, ensemble tout bleu, tout rose ou bleu et rose, selon l'humeur. Ainsi se déroulera le quadrille des hôtesses dans les cabines des Jets d'Air France dès la belle saison. En effet, le choix de la couleur de ses deux uniformes d'été appartient à l'hôtesse.

L'ensemble est en tergal flammé bleu ciel ou rose pastel de Lesur. Pour être assuré de conserver les mêmes tons au cours des ans, il a été teint une quantité de tissu égale à quatre ans de consommation en fil.

Deux poches se glissent dans les coutures des panneaux, légèrement biaisés, du devant de la jupe, que deux gros plis couchés rendent confortable. Le haut, qui se porte par dessus la jupe, a des petites manches courtes et une encolure dégagée au col fermé par un nœud chapelier en gros grain bleu marine.

Sur cet ensemble, qui ne fait pas uniforme, un original imperméable bleu marine 7/8, sans col, en nylon peau d'orange de Buccol, avec une martingale basse ornée de deux boutons en métal argenté.

La maison Montézin a créé la coiffure à visière qui, en hiver, se portera en taupé et l'été en tergal de laine. Un foulard de soie bleu et blanc, signé Balenciaga, des bottes montantes et des escarpins bleu marine de Darchamp, le sac modèle exclusif de Chi Chen Itza, et des gants blancs de Neyret composent les accessoires.

Quelques chiffres.

En 1969, il y aura 1 320 hôtesses à habiller, et les trois années suivantes, ce nombre augmentera régulièrement pour atteindre celui de 2 200, en 1972.

Givenchy says. "For three years before he closed, the Mar-·
quesa de Llanzol and Esparza and I were trying to persuade him not to." He was tired, he told Givenchy, but he
couldn't stop because he was supporting so many people—
presumably mostly his family—that he was afraid he
wouldn't have enough to live on if he retired. Couture houses
were closing and his own house was taking in less money.
In 1967—was it a sign of panic?—he let the press back in
to view his collection. Even Florette's order book shows a
decline, although she had as new clients girls from the
house of the famous procuress Mme Claude. "Just a few.
They were very pretty and very polite," she said. They
paid with checks signed by their customers, except for one
who gave cash. She must have been turning tricks on the
side to earn enough for the clothes, Florette guessed.

Designers, caught in the world of commerce, cannot afford
themselves a late style in the manner of painters and writers and composers, but in his 1967 collections Balenciaga
produced three almost ecstatic examples of what must be
called his late style: the four-sided "envelope" dress, the
"chou," with its deep black ruffle around the face that could
be lowered to the shoulders, and the coal scuttle bridal
gown. It was impossible, even for him, to go further, and
he closed his house the following year.

Diana Vreeland, staying with Mona Bismarck in Capri, got the news from Consuelo Crespi, who had just heard
it over the radio in Rome: "Mona didn't come out of her
room for three days. I mean, she went into a complete . . . I
mean it was the end of a certain part of her *life*."

The extraordinary "chou" dress of 1967

It was like the moment when Prospero abandons his magic, but it wasn't a moment. It was a sloppy, drawn-out, painful mess. Already on April 26, 1968, the London *Daily Express*'s Sam White announced BALENCIAGA DECIDES TO QUIT—AND FASHION WILL NEVER BE THE SAME AGAIN. Official denials followed, then on May 23, *The New York Times* stated, correctly, NOTHING LEFT TO ACHIEVE, BALENCIAGA CALLS IT A DAY. No one in the house, not even Mlle Renée, it is said, had been warned.

"He left like the *grand seigneur* that he was. He closed the door," Givenchy says. It was more brutal than grand. Perhaps to Balenciaga in Madrid the dramatic photos of the May events in Paris—the burning cars, the street fighting—seemed a replay of Spain's chaotic civil war: a sign, or a pretext, to close. He was tired, and he did.

On May 31, typewritten registered letters signed by Mlle Renée informed all four hundred employees that they had been fired. It might have been less painful had Balenciaga come back from Spain; as it was, Florette learned about the closing from a client who telephoned from New York to ask her to reserve a particular number from the collection since there wouldn't be another. "For years I felt a mixture of rage and sorrow," she said. Odette, cooler, said that some employees wanted to sue: "But the last collection was weak, we could see he was tired. His nephews pushed him to go on."

The little employees, Warhol's "makers of buttons," some of them already past retirement age, accepted their fate silently. Odette wrote a letter to Balenciaga thanking him for what she had learned from him, and a retired model was so upset she wrote him a poem. Florette got a pile of condolence letters from clients, most of them asking her where she would go next. Several addressed her as "Fleurette" and one interrupted her grief to ask Florette to cancel her hair appointment at Carita as she wouldn't be coming to Paris. "I shall very much miss my Balenciaga wardrobe," wrote Mrs. Angelika W. Frink of 610 Park Avenue, while Mary Lee Fairbanks, in bright green ink,

The last page of Florette's order book

```
ZCZC FEB217 WAA815
FRPA CO UIAW 022
TDW UPPERVILLE VA 22/20 24 1504 (CNT PCTN)



MLLE RENEE TAMISIER
C/O BALENCIAGA
10 AVENUE GEORGE V
PARISFRANCE


PENSE A VOUS AVEC BEAUCOUP D'AFFECTION . LOVE
    BUNNY MELLON



COLL 10 V
```

Condolence telegram from Bunny Mellon to Mlle Renée

reflected, "It is terribly sad that the one and only genius is retiring but he deserves peace and serenity. It leaves a great void in the world but he must be a man richly rewarded for his devotion to his knowledge, talent and compassion."

No one can give with accuracy the closing date of the house since orders had to be filled and the sad process dragged on for months. (The Spanish houses closed after Paris.) Danielle stayed until the last days, by which time Balenciaga was back. "Monsieur Balenciaga came into the *cabine* with Mademoiselle Renée and said, Take what you like, Danielle, this suit maybe or this dress. And each time Renée said, No, Monsieur, that's been sold. She was so hard and he was so generous." In what sounds like a total breakdown, Florette says that Renée left disordered piles of unsold garments around, hanging on to them or throwing them away: "Really, into the garbage bin. It was horrible. Monsieur Balenciaga didn't care by then." Renée's niece Claudia, an assistant vendeuse, says that despite their closeness she never spoke of the closing to her aunt and her aunt never brought it up. Renée, who had lived at 10 Avenue George V in a transformed attic, moved to Enghien, a nondescript former spa outside Paris, and died there in 1994. Odette, who decided at the age of fifty-five to marry a widower, chose a free wedding dress dating from the late 1940s, and hats for her five new stepchildren.

Florette took nothing, and after thirty-one years got as severance pay a sum just sufficient to repaint her one-bedroom apartment.

Balenciaga's staff was accustomed to the peremptory ways of genius so, once the shock had passed, none of them seemed to hold the way that he closed against him. They remained protective and over the years some of them came to resent the probing of strangers into what they regarded as the best years of their lives. "Monsieur Balenciaga was someone extraordinary about whom I do not wish to speak," a fitter named Jacqueline told me over the telephone. "My memories are in my heart and I don't want to share them with anyone." Understood, but had she known Florette? "I knew her very well, she was a vendeuse *et c'est tout.*" Click of the telephone being hung up. That wasn't really all, for Florette had shown me a note from Jacqueline written in 1968: "Dear Mme Florette, What I want to do in this letter is thank you, first of all for the courage you had when I began. You weren't afraid to work with me and from that I gained confidence. Thank you for continuing to believe in me, a thousand thanks . . ."

None of Balenciaga's employees had trouble finding work in other houses. Florette, with her winning ways and an order book worth its weight in gold, had her choice, and

"There was Chanel, Grès, Saint Laurent, whom I would have liked to go to but I didn't care for Monsieur Bergé," Florette said. "I told Monsieur Balenciaga I didn't know where to go and he said, You know, I am very fond of Monsieur de Givenchy, I advise you to go to him." Florette had had her doubts about Givenchy since the expulsion of M. Bizcarrondo, but Givenchy, she says, offered her the job of directrice and so she accepted. M. Bizcarrondo's widow asked her how she could do such a thing.

Odette and Danielle and several Balenciaga fitters also crossed the Avenue George V to work at Givenchy. "The vendeuses hated us. It was not a good ambience," Odette says.

"There was a lot of jealousy and ill-humor among the staff," said Florette. "The directrice refused to go and was odious." Eugenia Sheppard, describing Florette as the smiling vendeuse, wrote that her customers "have followed her, to the last woman." Maybe so, but she didn't see them: "I was stuck off in a little office and when my clients came in they were told I wasn't there." The position of directrice was never mentioned again.

Florette suspected, reasonably enough, that the point in hiring her had been simply to freeze her order book: to make her a nonperson. Mona Bismarck, whose Balenciaga vendeuse had retired and who should logically have been given to Florette when she moved to Givenchy, was handed on instead to the lesser talent of Odette—why, Odette never knew. It may be because she went to the private office of Givenchy after the directrice claimed, as she had with Florette, that her Balenciaga clients had been longtime Givenchy clients. "There's no point in my staying on here since all my clients already have vendeuses," Odette told him. She was given Mona and ended up staying at Givenchy for seventeen years, while Florette suffered through three years of humiliation and went home every night and cried.

The Givenchy years were her low point, but Florette, being Florette, picked herself up and soon, with André Courrèges, had a job where she had the best time in her life. She had known Courrèges at Balenciaga, where she admired his tailoring skill (she says he created several of Balenciaga's successful models, including the famous windowpane-check coat), and Courrèges had wanted her from the start. "I said, Your style isn't right for my clients. He said, I'll make clothes for your clients."

He started a couture line especially for her, modifying his space-age look for older, richer women. Florette was put in charge, having reassured the always prickly Coqueline Courrèges, whom she had known as a Balenciaga seamstress, that she would always address her as Madame when clients were around.

"It was nothing like Balenciaga," Florette said; "at Courrèges one could amuse oneself." But you amused yourself at Balenciaga, I remarked. "Yes, because it's my nature, but it wasn't very droll."

Florette cut off her brown chignon, becoming a windswept blonde, and wore Courrèges's gleaming dental-hygienist white instead of Balenciaga's black. For her clients, Courrèges began making a luxury line, including what she described as very good evening dresses with long sleeves. "I would tell Monsieur Courrèges what was needed and he always understood because we had worked together at Balenciaga." It was like a passport to youth: "Clients couldn't dress there completely, but still there was plenty for them." Among the new clients was the Baroness Guy de Rothschild; the Baroness Alain, on the other hand, never came, preferring Saint Laurent.

Being the directrice involved a good deal of PR work: prospecting for new clients at the court of the Shah of Iran and going to New York in, for example, a little black ("I didn't want to shock them in white") Courrèges dress and jacket that she would wear at lunch with clients at La Grenouille and wear again without the jacket when invited to their homes for dinner: "They were amazed that one could wear the same outfit night and day."

It may not have had the splendor of Balenciaga, but it was livelier, and it lasted until 1982. By then Florette was seventy-one years old, ready to be just Mme Chelot and to relieve Payot of the title M. Florette. In those days, the job of vendeuse was the only one in which women with no skills or diplomas could win excellent wages—by the time Balenciaga closed, Florette was earning more than a full professor at Harvard—but few vendeuses had a family life. That Florette had both was, she knew, thanks in part to Payot's familiarity with her working world and to his patience.

"At collection time she would come home in a state of nerves, trembling, lashing out, and she could be nasty," says Anita Delion, Florette's niece. "No one ever saw it. Payot calmed her down. He could be a little *vieille France*—he would argue about whether they really needed a washing machine, for example—but he was marvelous."

I saw Payot a few times and liked him a lot—a tall, slim, friendly man who spoke very precise English and had a very un-French taste for peanut butter. Since leaving work he had been writing mildly erotic novels. I counted fifteen leather-bound volumes, self-published, in the living room. Payot decided that as retirees they should sell the Normandy dream house, keep the Île St. Louis apartment, and rather conventionally buy a flat in Cannes, where Florette used Cécile de Rothschild's fine English gardening tools on her small new terrace. During the time that remained, Florette didn't see her Balenciaga friends or clients. "My husband said that's all over now. And he was right. No, he wasn't right, but he had put up with enough, no?" Payot died in Cannes from a heart attack in 1985 and Florette briefly lost her mind.

"I remember none of this but it seems I got through the funeral receiving everyone very charmingly, Monsieur Courrèges said, as if I were giving a cocktail party. Then at the church I lost it and kept saying, Where is Payot, tell him to hurry back, why is he so late? When I got home I sat there in my Balenciaga black dress and hat, took off my hat, and waited for him. I kept saying, Where is Payot, and not being able to find him." After a while, her nieces and nephews thought she should be sent away for psychiatric care, but her doctor said not to worry, she would pull out of it. And after two years, she did.

Florette was always a glass-is-half-full person, while Balenciaga was definitely a half-empty (or, more likely, was most concerned with the shape of the glass). She had almost twenty years left after Payot's death, and except for the last four months, she lived them very well. She took up with old Balenciaga friends again, including the mannequin Nicole Parent, who drove her home after lunch in her

Florette at 90

Morgan 4/4, and Jean-Claude Janet, widower of Balenciaga's window dresser; she made new ones such as the designer Azzedine Alaïa. And she installed a walk-in bathtub "for when I get old" (she was nearly ninety at the time). A month before falling ill, she called me from Cannes to say she had been swimming and was watching a horse show from her terrace. "The older I get, the more I want to live. It's odd, isn't it? It isn't that I'm afraid to die—I am not—it's just that I find life so wonderful that it's hard to leave."

All her life she retained that most attractive quality, a sense of wonder. Not because she was naïve—she certainly

was not—but because the wonderful had happened to her.
And so she never lost her curiosity. "I talk to everyone,"
she said. "I think people are surprised that at my age I am
so interested." I watched strangers' reactions to this lively
small woman (she said she had lost four inches in height
over the years) as she chatted to them in restaurants or
taxis, and they were always charmed. This in sullen Paris!
Even in her apartment building on the Île St. Louis, where
the concierge was banned from doing tenants' housework,
one of them, Mme Georges Pompidou, insisted that an exception be made: "If it's for Florette, it's all right."

She wore glasses only for reading, her hearing and brain
were in perfect order, her movements deft as she cut frozen
pizza with pinking shears during our taping sessions in
her Paris flat. She was very popular in Cannes, where she
spent the summers and went winter swimming in the
bleakest months, and she was bored stiff among the other
old folk. "I bring them something from the outside world.
When I arrive they look so sad that I start waking them up
and they say, Why don't you come more often? That would
amuse me not at all, they're all half asleep." She played gin
rummy twice a week and, although often asked, refused
to take any of the ladies shopping.

In Paris, her hair now short and white, she was chic in a
Balenciaga-like blouson cut from her long mink coat, and a
Courrèges pullover. She paid for a long ninetieth-birthday
cruise by selling her Balenciaga vendeuse outfits to Alaïa,
who also collected Vionnets; the few Balanciagas that she
had for her own use she would never sell. She admired
Alaïa ("I have watched him work, it was perfect, I think I
would have liked to work with him"), as she had Saint

Laurent ("a real creator"). She also liked Gaultier and surprised me by calling Lagerfeld "insignificant," which I finally realized meant he hasn't left a personal stamp on the couture: "He knows how to do everything. He knows how to take ideas and adapt them, which is already a great talent, don't you think?" she said. When I interrupted one of her Givenchy rants to say he had talent, she replied, "Talent, no. Taste, yes."

While we talked about being a vendeuse, I could see that she was developing a new perspective on the job. I don't think that earlier she would have said that vendeuses were a form of personal servant and I am sure she would not have announced one day, "Quite honestly, I did that job because I was put into the métier, but had I had the chance it isn't what I would have done. I think you have to make yourself care about it because it really isn't a very pleasant world."

Surely not, but she performed with a sort of glow that her favored clients remembered. One afternoon she asked the Baroness Alain if she might bring me to tea, and I was touched to see the closeness and affection between the two women, the differences in status so well understood that they became irrelevant. The baroness was tall, charming, and still beautiful; she had had a bad automobile accident four months earlier and was in a neck brace, which she concealed with a striped shirt collar worn with the wings turned up and a ribbon around her throat. Her jacket was black and her trousers red. I thought she looked like a Directoire dandy but Florette told me later that with that collar she looked like Lagerfeld.

The baroness talked about Balenciaga's leather-lined

elevator ("a very beautiful elevator, grand luxe") and the clear shadowless lighting of the salon. "I remember that lighting. Balenciaga knew how to live, how to place things, there was a great simplicity made from elements that were precious. It was serious because *la mode* was important then. Now it is important because it brings in a lot of money, while then it was important for itself and it was to be respected." She couldn't recall how she came to Florette but it was, she said, love at first sight. "She was *formidable* because she knew at once what one wanted, what one liked. It was easy with her, I didn't order ten or twelve dresses at a time like some people but she knew what I might need because she knew how I lived."

She spoke of her favorite Balenciagas—a beige lace evening gown over a flesh-colored base and a pink chiffon dotted in black. "And in the back there was a tiny velvet bow, really tiny. What was fascinating about it was just that little black velvet bow, so small among all that chiffon—that was what made it amusing." And she showed me, hanging in a corridor, the portrait by Balthus, painted in 1958, in which she wore a black Balenciaga coat: "Three months of sittings, every morning. I wouldn't have chosen anyone else."

The one regret, mildly expressed, was that Florette had never introduced her to Balenciaga, whom her sister-in-law Liliane had met at winter sports in Davos and talked about a lot. "He didn't want to see anyone," Florette replied, and the baroness said, "It's all right, it's just that it would have been nice." After we left I asked Florette why she hadn't made the introduction. "I could have, but I wasn't going to irritate him with clients," she said. "He

would have done it if I'd asked, he wasn't really *sauvage.*"
When I commented on the baroness's elegance, Florette
sighed, "Yes, but those red trousers!"

She did the same thing soon after when we went together to the Mona Bismarck Foundation in Paris for the
opening of an exhibition of Mona's Balenciagas curated by
Givenchy. It was slightly time-warp, filled with the sort of
formerly beautiful and still chic women in dark pantsuits
who clearly knew how to hold a cigarette, make graceful
hand gestures, have flings. Then Albina du Boisrouvray,
daughter of the "Frou-Frou"-singing countess, appeared
and she and Florette fell into each other's arms. Albina has
founded a worldwide charity for AIDS children in memory of her only son, killed in a helicopter crash, and funded
by the sale of her mother's jewels (for a reported $31.2
million) at Sotheby's, as well as her art collection and real
estate holdings. (Her mother's Balenciagas she gave to the
nuns next door who had been paid to pray for sun at the
countess's garden parties.) Albina's own interest in fashion,
in view of the life she leads, is minimal. For the Bismarck
show, Florette had spent thirty minutes on her makeup,
refused to check her mink blouson, and was wearing black
kid gloves "for Monsieur Balenciaga because he hated it if
we didn't wear gloves." She was delighted to see a few old
friends, "but my God, *la petite Boisrouvray,* did you see
how badly she was dressed!"

Givenchy's Bismarck Foundation show, which included
forty Balenciagas that Mona had left to him and seven bor-
rowed Balenciaga bridal gowns, was held in the spring of
2006, succeeded by a spurt of worldwide exhibitions. "For
the next four or five years there will be Balenciaga, Balenciaga, Balenciaga everywhere," Givenchy said.

The major event, shortly after the Bismarck show, was the first Balenciaga retrospective to be held in Paris— thirty-four years after his death—at the Musée des Arts Décoratifs. Florette threw herself into helping its young curator, Pamela Golbin, whom she liked very much, and, as one of the last survivors of the house of Balenciaga, was flooded by requests for interviews. She was on Spanish and Japanese television and enjoyed every minute of it. "Years ago, Payot had an astrologer do my chart and she said I would find fame in my old age. I never thought she would be right."

The Arts Décoratifs show opening, on July 5, 2006, was a glossy Parisian moment, attended by Mick Jagger, Hugh Grant, Martha Stewart, and a crowd of international fashion groupies. I went the next day with Florette, she, after much deliberation, having chosen to wear—it was a very hot day—a cap-sleeved Balenciaga dress in lime green shantung. She was vivacious and charming with the television cameramen, most of whom she knew by then, at the entrance but became increasingly quiet during the show. The taxi ride home passed in silence.

The show was perhaps a bit too stately, the dresses stiff. When I suggested to Florette that we go again, she refused and said she hadn't liked it at all: "Those glass cases, like coffins." Like coffins. She had given so much—too much—to bringing it all back and was saddened and bewildered that somehow none of it was right, was enough. It was all finally and fatally dead. And so, within a few months, was she.

The decline was rapid—she never even got to use her walk-in bathtub—and her physician proved unworthy of her longtime trust. "Doctor, you have let me down," she sadly told him. She, who was so meticulous, suffered from the medical disarray as much as the pain from what was probably a stomach cancer, and although she tried to be bright during visits, she was beyond consolation. I had to go to New York, and on November 16, 2006, I telephoned to wish her a happy birthday. Her niece, Anita, answered and said that Florette had died that morning. She had just turned ninety-five.

She was buried in Saint Cloud, next to her mother-in-law and Payot. Her squabbling nieces and nephews did not get together over the funeral announcements, which meant that Alaïa was invited to the ceremony but neither Benoît Gaubert, who had known her from childhood, nor her Balenciaga friends were even aware she had died.

8

Over the years, Balenciaga sent Florette picture postcards from Spain and, for the New Year, the traditional stiff white card with a stiff handwritten message. But one year he wrote, "What can I wish you, you who have everything?"

Perhaps this was just a reflection on her own completeness, perhaps there is a rueful suggestion of what he had missed because of the ravening demands of genius. Not that he would have used the word genius, just as he never used the word art about his work. His word was *métier*—skill, or trade—and the motor of his life was an exalted view of that work.

To Balenciaga, his work revealed God's hidden harmony, Father Robert Pieplu said when he delivered his funeral elegy on March 29, 1972, in the church just up the street from the Avenue Marceau apartment. Wearing the cassock Balenciaga had made for him, he urged his gathered friends to build a harmonious world through their own work.

In the winter world of retirement, Balenciaga had seemed lost. He dabbled in Madrid real estate, as he had since the 1950s, buying, developing, and selling apartment buildings. Givenchy says he would keep the penthouses for himself, spend one night, find the noise intolerable, and move on. He scoured Spanish stores for antique Cuenca carpets, piling them up in the Madrid flat that he finally chose so that, says Givenchy, they resembled the pastry called a mille-feuille.

An undated letter in his firm rolling script to the Marquesa de Llanzol in which he complains about the apprentices he was working with suggests that he may have had a project that was never realized, and he did make the occasional dress or modification (*la manga!*) with the help of his Madrid seamstresses, as well as the bridal gown for Generalissimo Franco's granddaughter. "Now I'm a housewife, a stand-in, a messenger boy and a bore," he wrote the marquesa, "but it is best that I realize all this and I am calmer but, at the same time, more annoyed."

The unsinkable Claudia Heard de Osborne tried to cheer him up in Madrid in 1969. "Cristóbal came every evening to the Ritz and dined with me. He looks good and is the same person. He and I always cry, though, before the evening is over." This he really didn't need.

Newly restless, he seems to have begun to travel. In a *Women's Wear* roundup after Balenciaga died, the New York designer Chester Weinberg recalled spending a few weeks with him the previous year in Greece: "The way he responded to antiquity was amazing—he was like a present-day extension of what we were looking at. He was a most gentle, simple, honest, creative man."

Givenchy refuses to believe that such a trip took place, but Weinberg had added a clinching detail: "He also made the best martinis."

When in Paris, Balenciaga kept up with his employees. He sent a note to the mannequin Danielle when she left Givenchy for Chanel in 1971 to wish her good luck. "How he heard about it I cannot guess," she said, "but how kind of him that was."

"One day after the house closed I ran into him, looking less soigné than usual," Florette told me. "He had let his hair get curly and he was carrying a long metal pot to cook fish in, he who never carried anything. He said he was going to cook a fish that night for friends. He seemed rather pleased with himself to be doing this and for carrying a package, but at the same time a bit embarrassed that I should see him."

He usually cut a distinguished figure in a sober dark suit relieved sometimes by a bow tie. Givenchy thinks his clothes were made in Spain. "I at that time dressed in London, at Huntsman, and was terribly pleased with myself. Obviously when I went to lunch with him I wore my latest from Huntsman. Cristóbal would say the fabric is good, but the sleeves! After lunch he would get on a stool, have his manservant bring a pair of scissors, and undo the sleeves. One day it was a camel hair jacket, another a camel hair coat. He said, You are too tall to wear a coat without a half-belt. He started to undo the hem to see if there was enough fabric, and there was. He gave me a raincoat to go home in. When he died, Gérard, his secretary, called and said, There are four or five ensembles in his workspace that are so big they must be yours, may I send them over to you? I found them with their sleeves just pinned and the coat with its undone hem. But that was Cristóbal."

He would often drop by Givenchy's studio and once

was turned away by an employee who failed to recognize him. Occasionally he would give advice. "One day," Givenchy said, "I was with a model named Beryl, a very pretty girl, and it was in the last days before the collection. I was working on the wedding dress, because you usually do that last, and I just couldn't get it right, I was so tired. Suddenly Cristóbal said, Suppose you did this, put that there? After two or three hours I saw the mannequin was beginning to fade and nothing was right—I think probably the design wasn't very good—and then Cristóbal said, Stop, just leave the dress as it was, it wasn't that bad. It will be perfectly all right and the other things I've seen are very pretty. Come back with me and have a dry martini." Givenchy had two.

After so many years of doing maybe 150 fittings a day, seated on a stool with his arms raised to the level of the mannequin, Balenciaga had problems with his back, and his fingers, because they were no longer at work, began to stiffen. "The doctor told him, You must get modeling clay and use your hands," Givenchy said. "Imagine, Balenciaga with modeling clay!"

Clearly at loose ends, he gave the only press interview of his life, choosing to speak with Prudence Glynn of the London *Times*, whom he had never met. Her short article, printed on August 3, 1971, was headed BALENCIAGA AND *LA VIE D'UN CHIEN*, a dog's life being how he viewed his trade: "Nobody knows what a hard métier it is, how killing is the work under all this luxury and glamour." The interview, which took place in his Paris apartment, is frustratingly short on quotes, but Glynn was totally charmed. He was, she says, tall and handsome and he smiled a lot: "The one thing I had never imagined this great austere figure to be was funny, but he is, and his eyes twinkle with spirit. He is not waspish and tells stories against himself equally easily." She quotes none of them but includes Balenciaga's praise of the recently deceased Chanel, ranking her at the top with Vionnet and the now forgotten house of Louise-boulanger. "Chanel took all the chi-chi and fuss out of women's clothing," he said.

He had attended Chanel's funeral a few months earlier, and the following year, on March 23, 1972, his own attenuated existence ended after a sudden heart attack in Javea, Spain. The news made the front page of *The New York Times*.

Givenchy flew to the burial in Getaria with his companion Philippe Venet and Emanuel Ungaro in an aircraft chartered by Balenciaga's fabric manufacturer friend, Gustav Zumsteg, and at the graveside he found the Marquesa de Llanzol, her daughter Sonsoles Díez de Rivera, Ramón Esparza, and the Balenciaga family. Most probably Balenciaga had gone to see about buying property on the Costa Blanca when he was stricken. It seems unconscionable that a seventy-seven-year-old man would not have left a will, but Balenciaga did not, or, as some people darkly say, a will was never found.

In a version contested by the Balenciaga family, Sonsoles Díez de Rivera says that on his last trip, Balenciaga went to a notary on his way to Altea, near Javea, wrote a will in which he left everything to Esparza, and said he would sign the will upon returning from Altea. Since he never returned there was no will, and his family became his sole heirs.

The modest Esparza, left in the cold, sued the family

unsuccessfully and was sufficiently embittered when he died in 1997 to leave his slim archive to New York's Fashion Institute of Technology rather than to a Spanish institution. It was a sad end for someone who had been at Balenciaga's side for more than twenty years. "He was always with him," Sonsoles says. "He helped Balenciaga a lot, I suppose, but he was very limited because after Balenciaga died when Esparza came to Madrid and called my mother she would always immediately send him to me—I can't stand him, she would say, I can't understand what Cristóbal saw in him, he's boring, he has no conversation."

A newer, less civil era began: Balenciaga without Balenciaga. Although he had told Givenchy and others that he wanted his name to die with him, the family decided otherwise and in time he became a brand, a word that he would not even have recognized. It began when the family decided to continue the Spanish operation with ready-to-wear, perfumes, and accessories under the leadership of Balenciaga's niece, Manuela. To a degree it was a reasonable decision since Balenciaga's brother, Juan Martín, and several of Juan Martín's children (he had nine) had been working in the Spanish houses during Balenciaga's lifetime. According to a grandnephew, Agustín Medina Balenciaga, a management consultant in his early fifties, they are a very close-knit clan sharing a certain remoteness, deep Catholicism, and nimble hands.

Balenciaga's beloved house in Igueldo burned down in about 1985 as a result of what Agustín says was probably an electric fault inflamed by layers of wax on its well-polished furniture. The properties in France and Spain were sold, as were the Cuenca rugs. Some personal effects remained in the family (Agustín has a lamp from Igueldo on his desk) and while the Braque and a Giacometti drawing were sold at Sotheby's Monaco, Balenciaga's paintings by Bernard Buffet were kept by his heirs. (Why on earth Balenciaga owned works by this painter who was merely fashionable is one of his many mysteries. He even broke his no-gifts rule and gave a yellow sari to Buffet's wife, Annabel, to wear to a Lido opening. Unfortunately, Elizabeth Taylor attended the same event in the same sari, and she had paid for hers.)

The post-Cristóbal ready-to-wear line was designed in Madrid and it failed to make waves. In 1978 a German company bought the perfume and ready-to-wear rights, according to Agustín, and in 1982 bought the rest. Ultimately the Balenciaga name was bought by Gucci, and when that company was taken over by the French tycoon François Pinault, it became part of his vast PPR empire. "It is true that it was a pain in our heart, we thought that Balenciaga would not like selling his name," Agustín says. "But we were the inheritors, it was our business, too."

Under Cristóbal, so obsessed by privacy, the house of Balenciaga seemed like *Hamlet* without the prince; now it is *Hamlet* without Hamlet. The name, depersonalized, is world famous thanks to urgent brand management. "Brand recognition is the vital issue," as the fashion editor Suzy Menkes, the sharpest observer of the scene, wrote in the *International Herald Tribune* in March 2010, adding a couple of months later, "the era of the star designer picked to create buzz and shake up the system in a venerable house is over."

In other words, the designer is expendable: the pen that

signs a licensing contract is more powerful than the well-placed pin.

The one designer unbowed by brand management is Karl Lagerfeld, the astute whirligig who has moved beyond product to become a brand himself. He is not only creative director of the house of Chanel, he is KARL, a living logo whose carefully etched black-and-white silhouette is chased for autographs on every continent and applauded by passersby on Mercer Street in SoHo. "I don't want to be real in people's minds," he stated in a 2007 biopic by Rodolphe Marconi. "I want to be an apparition." One such apparition is on a Karl teddy bear made by Steiff in 2008. His designs, often illustrated by a stylized self-portrait, range from pens to Diet Coke bottles to sneakers to an inexpensive Karl fashion collection available only online. He publishes books, takes photographs, made newspaper drawings for France's last presidential campaign, and did the commentary on French TV for Prince William's wedding. There is no conflict between Brand Karl and his day job because *he* is his day job, and there are surely more people in the world today who know Karl's name than Coco Chanel's.

At Balenciaga, Nicolas Ghesquière, born three years after the house closed in 1968, triumphantly put it back on the map, telling *Women's Wear Daily*, "My greatest challenge is to make Balenciaga a brand and to give the feeling that we can feed the stores like a brand" (March 1, 2005). By the time Ghesquière left late in 2012, Balenciaga had sixty-two branches, including eleven in China, and there is good reason to hope the number will increase under his successor Alexander Wang, with his Korean blood and downtown New York smarts. Like Ghesquière, Wang had studied the Balenciaga archive (it is now respectable, even fashionable, to copy, quote, or in current parlance to "reference" past designers), and to a degree the influence of Balenciaga can be seen in other designers as well. "I think that the sculpted style of Balenciaga has had a certain revival," Menkes says, "but not in the same way, firstly because you cannot get the same effect of stand-away tailoring in ready-to-wear because the whole point is that it follows the contours of a specific body. Secondly because in this body-conscious era, the idea of clothes that create a 'bubble' around the female form does not seem quite right. But the nobility of Balenciaga and the big gestures are interesting for designers to follow using new high-tech fabrics."

In 1973, when Diana Vreeland launched her Balenciaga show at the Metropolitan Museum, the *New York Times* headline said THE ERA OF BALENCIAGA: IT SEEMS SO LONG AGO, and Calvin Klein was quoted as remarking, "Most of it looks out of date." In the strictest sense it is, in a day when plastic surgery replaces sculptural scissors, when glitz trumps allure, when the fake becomes desirable if it is termed *faux*, when Balenciaga's severe Spanish word *cursi* connotes something merely twee, and when Tom Ford can tell London's *Sunday Times*, as he did in 2008, "Over the years I've learnt that all this stuff we do is a bunch of crap."

The renewed interest in Balenciaga these days is thanks in part to Ghesquière's headline making—$101,370 one season for an evening dress—and to his marketing savvy in making a handbag the key fashion accessory with his "It Bags," said in 2006 to account for 35 percent of the house's earnings. That same year he co-curated the long-overdue

Balenciaga retrospective in Paris (coolly taking one floor of the exhibition space for himself). So, ironically, Balenciaga is back on the map, even if most people have never heard of Cristóbal, and more marketable than in his lifetime.

The cherry on the cake was the opening in the summer of 2011 of a museum devoted entirely to Balenciaga in his home village, Getaria. Long delayed by an embezzling former mayor who gave the commission to his architect boyfriend and caused several accessories to disappear, the opening was attended by Queen Sofía of Spain and the international press. The museum, located in a hefty glass addition to the home of Balenciaga's first patron, the Marquesa de Casa Torres, and curated by Miren Arzalluz, has twelve hundred Balenciagas dating back to 1912, which will be shown in rotation in six-month-long exhibitions. Givenchy served as founding president, donated many of the clothes, and got such friends as Bunny Mellon to contribute over two dozen more. Sonsoles Díez de Rivera also gave all her Balenciagas, but only on loan. "I keep them there as if it were my cupboard, that way I can get them if I want to wear them," she said.

Getaria had prepared for the museum by finally putting up the plaque to mark Balenciaga's birthplace, and the current mayor reckons that, like Frank Gehry's Bilbao museum, it will bring many tourists. In museum entrance fees, books, and obviously as merchandise, Balenciaga sells. It is a world counter to everything he lived and expressed in his clothes, but perhaps he would be pleased that instead of just a handful of rich clients and fashion editors, young people at exhibitions all over the world can now marvel at his work, can see the richness of his imagination and the rigor of his technique, can sense the probity behind the grand gesture. "When he left the world of haute couture, something stopped, perhaps a way of writing with scissors and cloth," said the master embroiderer François Lesage.

For some today, Balenciaga will be a fashion discovery; for others he is more precious. When I asked Albina du Boisrouvray, the former client who now devotes herself to children living in misery, why she had troubled to go to the Bismarck Foundation show in 2006, she replied, "One needs to replenish the sense of beauty, harmony, and lightness in order to heal the soul. That is why I went."

Balenciaga has been called a visionary, which in its proper meaning has nothing to do with seeing the future: in its true old sense it suggests imagining the impossible. Balenciaga made the impossible possible, if for what could only be a brief time. His clothes do not evoke nostalgia because nostalgia is a lightweight emotion, but they do inspire respect, a nearly unknown word in the throwaway world of fashion. With respect goes, somehow, a degree of hope, as John Berger says at the start of this story: "the supposition that, despite everything, a melody can be looked for and sometimes found." Balenciaga, François Lesage thought, had put a touch of eternity into his work.

Cristóbal Balenciaga in 1962

NOTES

PROLOGUE

3   *"the master of us all"*: Cathy Horyn, "When Paris Was All That Mattered," *New York Times*, July 6, 2006.

3   *"Do not waste yourself"*: Musée Historique des Tissus, *Hommage à Balenciaga* exhibition catalog, Lyons, 1986, 38.

3   *He was, says*: John B. Fairchild to author, New York, 2010.

4   *when Louis XIV's finance minister*: Valerie Steele, *Paris Fashion: A Cultural History* (Oxford: Oxford University Press, 1988), 23.

4   toilettes politiques: Lucien François, *Comment un Nom Devient une Griffe* (Paris: Gallimard, 1961), 17.

4   *Barthes, whose article on Chanel*: Roland Barthes, *The Language of Fashion*, translated by Andy Stafford (Oxford: Berg, 2006), 107.

5   *in 1936 a policeman refused*: Eugen Weber, *The Hollow Years: France in the 1930s* (New York: W. W. Norton, 1994), 85.

5   *(it has been estimated . . .)*: *Hommage à Balenciaga*, 122.

5   *"If a woman came in"*: Diana Vreeland, *D.V.* (New York: Knopf, 1984), 106.

6   *when his close friend Hubert de Givenchy*: Hubert de Givenchy to author, May 2006. All Givenchy quotations are from this interview and another in October 2010.

6   *Mrs. Paul ("Bunny") Mellon*: Letter to Renée Tamisier, 1968, Balenciaga archive, Paris.

6   *Gloria Guinness wondered*: Metropolitan Museum of Art, *The World of Balenciaga*, Metropolitan Museum exhibition catalog, 1973, 15.

6   *Claudia Heard de Osborne*: Myra Walker, *Balenciaga and His Legacy* (New Haven: Yale University Press, 2006), 53.

6   *Pauline de Rothschild*: *World of Balenciaga*, 19.

7   *a collaborator remembers*: *Hommage à Balenciaga*, 42.

7   *Only a few years ago*: Lesley Ellis Miller to author, London, 2005.

8 *Florette Chelot, his top vendeuse:* Florette Chelot to author. All Florette Chelot quotations are from interviews 2004–2006.

I

11 *a contemporary poet:* Richard Sieburth to author, e-mail, 2010.

11 *"In the center of a street":* World of Balenciaga, 18.

12 *a young Basque curator:* Miren Arzalluz, *Cristóbal Balenciaga: The Making of a Master (1895–1936)* (London: V&A Publishing, 2011), passim.

14 *three existential questions:* Paddy Woodworth, *The Basque Country: A Cultural History* (Oxford: Signal Books, 2007), 9, 13, 14.

14 *The Basques' language:* Ibid., 9.

16 *one of his models was astonished:* Danielle Slavik to author, Paris, 2008.

17 *a lifelong friendship with Madeleine Vionnet:* All Vionnet quotes are from author's interview, 1966.

19 *"no one has carried the art":* Cecil Beaton, *The Glass of Fashion* (Garden City, NY: Doubleday, 1954), 295.

22 *by the age of twenty-one:* Hamish Bowles, *Balenciaga: Spanish Master* (exhibition catalog) (New York: Skira/Rizzoli, 2010), 6.

24 *The economy, mismanaged:* Anthony Beevor, *The Battle for Spain: The Spanish Civil War 1936–1939* (London: Phoenix, 2006), 18–20; Hugh Thomas, *The Spanish Civil War* (London: Penguin, 1965), 186.

24 *Europe's youngest general:* Paul Preston, *Franco: A Biography* (New York: Basic Books, 1994), xviii.

25 *Franquists used live bodies:* Beevor, *Battle for Spain*, 73.

25 *whom Vogue's Bettina Ballard:* Bettina Ballard, *In My Fashion* (Philadelphia: David McKay, 1960), 110. Unless otherwise noted, all Ballard quotations are from this book.

27 *She refused on the grounds:* Edmonde Charles-Roux, *Chanel and Her World* (London: Weidenfeld & Nicolson, 1981), 208.

27 *"It was this that made the thirties":* Janet Flanner, foreword, *Salute to the Thirties* (London: Bodley Head, 1971), 4.

34 *(As Gloria Guinness later pointed out . . .):* World of Balenciaga, 16.

34 *"They walk with a pleasant swagger":* Women's Journal, September, 1939.

36 *The former Renée Bousquet:* Renée Le Roux to author, 1986 and 2004.

38 *Diana Vreeland, writing to "Darling Mona":* Letter, April 23, 1973, Filson Historical Society, Louisville, Kentucky.

38 *Marie-Andrée Jouve:* Marie-Andrée Jouve and Jacqueline Demornex, *Balenciaga* (London: Thames & Hudson), 1989, passim.

38   *Oscar de la Renta*: Oscar de la Renta to author, New York, 2010. De la Renta had gone to Spain in the early 1950s to study art and found work at Balenciaga making sketches to send to clients, which is done today with videos. The Madrid house, he says, was as forbidding as the one in Paris, and he was terrified whenever Balenciaga passed. Told by Balenciaga that he would need another year in Spain before being ready to move to the Paris house, he left and joined the house of Castillo.

39   *As Pamela Golbin*: Pamela Golbin to author, Paris, 2006.

41   *"Don't order that"*: Sonsoles Díez de Rivera to author, telephone, 2010.

41   *Balenciaga's own private collection*: *Cristóbal Balenciaga Collectioneur de Modes* exhibition catalog, Musée Galliera, 2012.

41   *"I found the clothes very pretty"*: Ballard, *In My Fashion*, 110.

42   *"Knowing journalists"*: Madge Garland, *The Indecisive Decade: The World of Fashion and Entertainment in the Thirties* (London: Macdonald, 1968), 125.

2

43   *Gloria Rubio*: Obituary, *The Times* (London), January 26, 1962.

45   *The great Paris World's Fair*: Shanny Peer, *France on Display* (Albany: State University of New York Press, 1998), 40; Piers Brendon, *The Dark Valley: A Panorama of the 1930s* (New York: Knopf, 2000), 576–79.

45   *For the writer Michel Leiris*: Peer, *France on Display*, 47.

45   *"we loved the dirndl"*: *Paris Fashion*, edited by Ruth Lyman (London: Michael Joseph, 1972), 107.

45   *Looking back, Madge Garland*: Garland, *Indecisive Decade*, 125.

46   *Cecil Beaton declared*: *Shots of Style: Great Fashion Photographs Chosen by David Bailey*, exhibition catalog, Victoria and Albert Museum, 1985, 24.

48   *Maurice Privat's annual forecast*: *1940 Prédictions Mondiales: Année de Grandeur Française* (Paris: Editions Medicis, 1940), passim.

48   *What sort of war*: Simone de Beauvoir, *The Prime of Life* (London: Penguin Books, 1962), 402.

48   *For fear of foreign spies*: Ibid., 384, and Ballard, *In My Fashion*, 150.

48   *Edna Woolman Chase*: Ballard, *In My Fashion*, 146.

49   *Schiaparelli built muffs*: Weber, *Hollow Years*, 266.

49   *the dowdy wife of France's military leader*: Dominique Veillon, *La Mode sous l'Occupation* (Paris: Payot, 1990), 29.

52   *General Gamelin, hero of*: Weber, *Hollow Years*, 256, 273.

52   *reliable carrier pigeons*: Ibid., 255–56.

52   *the first government minister to flee Paris*: Herbert Lottman, *The Fall of Paris, June 1940* (London: Sinclair-Stevenson, 1992), 228.

52   *"What is the worst thing"*: Weber, *Hollow Years*, 24.

52   *As Robert O. Paxton*: Robert O. Paxton, *Vichy France: The Old Guard and the New Order* (New York: Columbia University Press, 1972), 227.

53   *Sometimes the work was*: Michael R. Marrus and Robert O. Paxton, *Vichy France and the Jews* (New York: Schocken Books, 1983), 263.

53   *"I used my power as a shield"*: Paxton, *Vichy France*, 358.

53   *"Abandoned populations"*: Thomas Kernan, *France on Berlin Time* (Philadelphia: J. B. Lippincott, 1941), 13.

54   *"With a regiment of young men"*: Ernst Jünger, *Journaux de Guerre* (Paris: Julliard, 1990), 455.

54   *the Germans made their first major move*: Nearly all the information on the German takeover of the haute couture comes from two sources, Dominique Veillon's *La Mode sous l'Occupation* and a typed manuscript by Lucien Lelong held by the Chambre Syndicale de la Haute Couture and translated by Susan Train. Lelong's manuscript was clearly written to explain and defend the couture before the courts that had been hastily set up to hear and judge accusations of collaboration with the Germans. No one in the couture, according to Veillon (230), was charged.

55   *according to Prince Jean-Louis de Faucigny-Lucinge*: Jean-Louis de Faucigny-Lucinge to author, 1987.

55   *"There was a social custom"*: Marcel Haedrich, *Coco Chanel: Her Life and Secrets* (New York: Little, Brown, 1972), 190.

58   *Christian Dior said to his friend*: Pierre Balmain, *My Years and Seasons* (London: Cassell, 1964), 78.

59   *"They thought I was Irish"*: Baroness Alain de Rothschild to author, Paris, 2006.

59   *Carmel Snow's fitter*: Penelope Rowlands, *A Dash of Daring: Carmel Snow and Her Life in Fashion, Art and Letters* (New York: Atria Books, 2005), 312.

60   *In the only interview*: Prudence Glynn, *The Times* (London), August 3, 1971.

63   *"The mental malnutrition"*: *Lee Miller's War*, edited by Anthony Penrose (New York: Condé Nast Books, 1992), 111.

64   *The Germans set back Paris clocks*: In the murky Occupation period even the question of whether the Germans set clocks ahead or back is unclear, further complicated by the fact that the Germans were on summer time, which France had not yet adopted. A man who lived through the period and the historian Richard Cobb in *French and*

Germans, Germans and French (Boston: Brandeis University Press, 1983), 132, both maintain that clocks were set ahead by one hour, but I have preferred Thomas Kernan's version (*France on Berlin Time*, 21) since he was writing at the start of the Occupation.

64 *"The entire gait"*: *Lee Miller's War*, 69.

65 *Christian Dior wrote in his memoirs*: Christian Dior, *Dior by Dior* (London: Penguin Books, 1958), 4.

65 *a respected British historian adds*: Anthony Beevor and Artemis Cooper, *Paris After the Liberation: 1944–1949* (London: Penguin Books, 1995), 305.

65 *"I am not unhappy here"*: Frederic Spotts, *The Shameful Peace: How French Artists and Intellectuals Survived the Nazi Occupation* (New Haven: Yale University Press, 2008), 21.

65 *Young Philippe Jullian*: Philippe Jullian, *Journal 1949–50* (Paris: Grasset, 2009), 54.

66 *One morning, two men*: Laurence Benaïm, *Marie Laure de Noailles: La Vicomtesse du Bizarre* (Paris: Grasset, 2001), 321.

66 *"The victory would efface"*: Simone de Beauvoir, *Force of Circumstance* (London: Penguin Books, 1968), 12.

66 *"It is not that France had behaved the worst"*: Tony Judt, *Postwar: A History of Europe Since 1945* (London: William Heinemann, 2005), 815.

68 *Carmel Snow, worried about competition*: Rowlands, *Dash of Daring*, 300ff.

69 *"I enjoyed seeing my name"*: Beauvoir, *Force of Circumstance*, 24–46.

70 *Le Théâtre de la Mode*: *Théâtre de la Mode, Fashion Dolls: The Survival of the Haute Couture*, edited by Susan Train and Eugène Clarence Braun-Munk (Portland, OR: Palmer/Pletsch Publishing, 2002).

3

73 *"We felt we had a right"*: Marie-France Pochna, *Christian Dior: The Biography* (New York: Overlook Duckworth, 2008), 165. Much of the material on Dior comes from this book and from Dior's memoir, *Dior by Dior*.

74 *when the wearer of a crinolined ballgown*: Pochna, *Christian Dior*, 185.

74 *"I loved, loved, loved"*: Polly Mellen to author, telephone, New York, 2010.

74 *who looked, according to Cecil Beaton*: Beaton, *Glass of Fashion*, 292.

74 *(Jacques Fath ...)*: Lyman, *Paris Fashion*, 177.

76 *(Dior is said to have exempted ...)*: Ibid., 148.

77   *Within days, a crusty old member*: Beevor and Cooper, *Paris After the Liberation*, 314.

77   *By 1949 the house of Dior*: *The Golden Age of Couture: Paris and London 1947–57*, exhibition catalog, Victoria and Albert Museum, 2008.

77   *"We waited each year"*: Ellen Melinkoff, *What We Wore: An Offbeat Social History of Women's Clothing, 1950 to 1980* (Whitby: Quill, 1984), 27.

78   *Dior himself said*: Lesley Ellis Miller, *Balenciaga* (London: V&A Publishing, 2007), 16.

78   *which Balenciaga refused to do*: Balenciaga was known to break his ban on lending or giving dresses, and during the wan postwar period Mlle Renée lent or gave steep reductions to good-looking and well-connected young Americans. Among the beneficiaries were Rosamond Bernier, then starting off at *Vogue*; Maggi Nolan, who had a social column at the Paris edition of the *New York Herald Tribune*; and Susan Mary Alsop, who paid $50 for the dress she wore to host Paris's first postwar ball, at the Pré Catalan (Susan Mary Alsop, *To Marietta from Paris* [New York: Doubleday, 1994], 82–3].

78   *At Balenciaga collections*: Susan Train to author, Paris, 2010.

78   *Dior was social theater*: Rosamond Bernier to author, New York, 2009.

79   *his mother was photographed*: *Vogue*, December 15, 1948.

80   *"Esparza was very nice"*: Luc Bouchage to author, Paris, 2006.

83   *In 1951 only one French household*: Judt, *Postwar*, 339.

84   *In the space of one spring afternoon*: Ned Rorem, *The Paris and New York Diaries of Ned Rorem 1951–1961* (Berkeley, CA: North Point Press, 1983), 6, 118.

86   *Bousquet had glommed on to the Brooks*: Natasha Parry and Peter Brook to author, Paris, 2009.

88   *"Only he is capable of cutting material"*: Miller, *Balenciaga*, 16.

90   *(John Fairchild says he saw her draw blood . . .)*: John B. Fairchild to author, 2010.

90   *The two friends fell out dramatically*: Givenchy's verbatim account says a lot about the personalities involved and illustrates the problem of pinning down facts concerning Balenciaga. There is no doubt that the rift occurred, possibly because of a Chanel interview in *Le Figaro* saying he was too old to continue in business but not mentioning his homosexuality, possibly because of gossip by Balenciaga's close friend Marie-Louise Bousquet (when in doubt it is always wise to blame Bousquet). But the *WWD* interview referred to by Givenchy, which he told me again he had seen with his own eyes (April 12, 2012), never existed according to John Fairchild (November 12, 2010) and to *WWD*'s editor, James Fallon, who kindly instituted a search of the archive for me. As for Balenciaga's returning all of Chanel's

gifts, the only known interview with him, in *The Times* (August 3, 1971), has Balenciaga praising her talent and mentioning that he has in his apartment "the most enchanting bronze duck, a gift from Cocò Chanel." The duck, according to Agustín Medina Balenciaga, Cristóbal's grandnephew, is still in the family's hands.

4

95 *One evening, gazing disconsolately*: Jouve and Demornex, *Balenciaga*, 55–56.

98 *Jean-Claude, who died at the age of ninety*: Jean-Claude Janet to author, Paris, 2006.

100 *"They all hated each other"*: Odette Sourdel to author, Paris, 2009.

104 *There were ten ateliers*: *Balenciaga Paris*, exhibition catalog, edited by Pamela Golbin, Musée de la Mode et Textiles (Arts Décoratifs museum at the Louvre), 2006, 19.

106 *Balenciaga would hire only untrained seamstresses*: Golbin, *Balenciaga Paris*, 19–20.

107 *"Yes, it was a hard place"*: Coqueline Courrèges to author, Paris, 2006.

109 *Nicole Parent, who stayed only a couple of years*: Nicole Parent to author, Paris, 2007.

113 *whom Truman Capote called Swans*: Truman Capote, *A Capote Reader* (London: Abacus, 1989), 551.

113 *Mona Bismarck, as she had recently become*: James D. Birchfield, *Kentucky Countess: Mona Bismarck in Art and Fashion* (Louisville: University of Kentucky Art Museum, 1997). Unless otherwise indicated, this is the source of Mona Bismarck information.

114 *"Mona was loyal"*: Gore Vidal to author, Paris, 2009.

117 *her second-floor suite at the Ritz*: C. David Heymann, *Poor Little Rich Girl: The Life and Legend of Barbara Hutton* (New York: Lyle Stuart, 1983), 33, 128.

118 *(Yves Saint Laurent's annual salary . . .)*: *International Herald Tribune*, March 21, 2012.

121 *according to her daughter, Albina*: Albina du Boisrouvray to author, Paris, 2010.

126 *Karl Lagerfeld, then a German teenager*: Karl Lagerfeld, "The Moving Image," *Vogue*, March 2000.

128 *One day, when Carmel Snow was having lunch*: Carmel Snow and Mary Louise Aswell, *The World of Carmel Snow* (New York: McGraw Hill, 1962), 167.

140 *Bizcarrondo, his great-niece says*: Dominique Caillois to author, telephone, 2009.

5

142   *His colors became more and more brilliant:* Vreeland, *D.V.,* 106, 107.

149   *In her 1956 book:* Célia Bertin, *Paris à la Mode* (New York: Harper, 1957), 226.

149   *At least two French fashion chroniclers:* Didier Grumbach, *Histoires de la Mode* (Paris: Seuil, 1993), 83; François, *Comment un Nom Devient une Griffe,* 143.

153   *"Balenciaga is such a trying man":* John Fairchild, *The Fashionable Savages* (Garden City, NY: Doubleday, 1965), 152.

153   *many of her clothes were in a train wreck:* Valentine Abdy, *Mona Bismarck, Cristóbal Balenciaga,* exhibition catalog, Mona Bismarck Foundation, 2006, 51.

153   *His biggest client of all:* Ibid., 58.

153   *Claudia Heard de Osborne:* Walker, passim.

154   *Sonsolita, as she was called:* Sonsoles Díez de Rivera to author, 2011.

158   *Danielle Slavik, blond and somewhat shy:* Danielle Slavik to author, 2010.

160   *When a young assistant:* Claudia Verbaum to author, telephone, 2011.

163   *says Benoît Gaubert:* Benoît Gaubert to author, 2008.

167   *The first was Schiaparelli:* Elsa Schiaparelli to author, 1965.

168   *When her goddaughter asked:* Madeleine Chapsal, *La Chair de la Robe* (Paris: Fayard, 1989), 188.

6

171   *by 1967 there were more than two thousand:* Judt, *Postwar,* 396.

171   *a book called* Elegance: Geneviève Antoine Dariaux, *Elegance* (Garden City, NY: Doubleday, 1964).

172   *Emanuel Ungaro:* Lauren Milligan, *Vogue.com,* April 19, 2010.

172   *The same year,* WWD *published: Women's Wear Daily,* January 25, 1965.

173   *inspiring Cecil Beaton to praise: International Herald Tribune,* August 25, 1967.

173   *The photographer David Bailey: International Herald Tribune,* October 15, 1985.

174   *"a forceful reminder of the speed":* Kennedy Fraser, *The Fashionable Mind: Reflections on Fashion, 1970–1982* (Boston: David R. Godine / Nonpareil, 1985), 84.

176   *"He understood his times":* film by Pierre Thoretton, *Yves Saint Laurent–Pierre Bergé, l'Amour fou,* 2010.

176   *Saint Laurent mentioned Balenciaga's technique: Women's Wear Daily,* March 27, 1972.

176   *Bergé claimed to have dined:* Laurence Benaïm, *Yves Saint Laurent* (Paris: Grasset, 2002), 135.

177   *on holiday in Marrakesh*: Alicia Drake, *The Beautiful Fall* (London: Bloomsbury, 2006), 60.

180   *Diana Vreeland, staying with Mona Bismarck*: Vreeland, *D.V.*, 107.

7

187   *"Monsieur Balenciaga was someone extraordinary"*: Jacqueline Ruotte to author, telephone, 2010.

188   *Eugenia Sheppard, describing Florette*: International Herald Tribune, August 1, 1968.

190   *"At collection time"*: Anita Delion to author, 2010.

194   *The baroness talked about*: Baroness Alain de Rothschild to author, 2006.

196   *Then Albina du Boisrouvray*: People, January 17, 1994.

8

199   *To Balenciaga, his work revealed*: Father Robert Pieplu, *The World of Balenciaga*, exhibition catalog, 10.

200   *An undated letter*: Archive, Balenciaga Museum, Getaria, Spain.

200   *The unsinkable Claudia*: Walker, *Balenciaga and His Legacy*, 46.

200   *the New York designer Chester Weinberg*: Women's Wear Daily, March 27, 1972.

202   *Prudence Glynn*: "Balenciaga and *la vie d'un chien*," The Times (London), August 3, 1971.

204   *they are a very close-knit clan*: Agustín Medina Balenciaga to author, telephone, 2011.

205   *(Why on earth Balenciaga owned works . . .)*: Givenchy, on April 12, 2012, gave me an explanation for Balenciaga's collection of paintings by Buffet. Balenciaga liked the boyish figure of Buffet's wife, Annabel, and each time he gave her a dress, Buffet (the former lover of Pierre Bergé) gave him a painting.

206   *biopic by Rodolphe Marconi*: Lagerfeld Confidential, 2007.

207   *"I think that the sculpted style"*: Suzy Menkes to author, e-mail, 2011.

207   *In 1973, when Diana Vreeland launched*: New York Times, March 23, 1973.

207   *when Tom Ford can tell*: The Sunday Times (London), January 31, 2010.

207   *$101,370 one season for an evening dress*: Vogue, July 2006.

207   *35 percent of the house's earnings*: Le Point, March 30, 2006.

209   *"When he left the world of haute couture"*: Bismarck Foundation catalog, 63.

209   *When I asked Albina*: Albina du Boisrouvray to author, e-mail, 2011.

ACKNOWLEDGMENTS

The most useful book on Balenciaga's Spanish years is *Cristóbal Balenciaga: The Making of a Master (1895–1936)* by Miren Arzalluz (2011) and, for the Paris years, Pamela Golbin's *Balenciaga Paris* (2006). Also helpful is the first major study, *Balenciaga* by Marie-Andrée Jouve and Jacqueline Demornex (1989), as are *Balenciaga* by Lesley Ellis Miller (2007) and *Balenciaga: Spanish Master* by Hamish Bowles (2010). For a memoir of Paris fashion from the 1930s to the 1950s, Bettina Ballard's *In My Fashion* (1960) is excellent. Part of my material appeared, in different form, in the April 2007 issue of *Vogue*.

My agent, Bill Clegg, put me in the skilled and friendly hands of Farrar, Straus and Giroux, so my thanks go to him and to Jonathan Galassi, Courtney Hodell, Mark Krotov, Charlotte Strick, Jonathan Lippincott, and Jeff Seroy.

I am also deeply grateful to Samuel Abt, Miren Arzalluz, Rosamond Bernier, Luc Bouchage, Peter Brook, Elizabeth Coll, Anita Delion, Sonsoles Díez de Rivera, John B. Fairchild, Lucien Frydlender, Benoît Gaubert, Hubert de Givenchy, Pamela Golbin, Robert Gottlieb, Immaculada de Habsburgo, Ian Hassett, Jean-Claude Janet, Janet Johnson,

Marie-Andrée Jouve, Brigitte Lacombe, Agustín Medina Balenciaga, Polly Mellen, Suzy Menkes, Lesley Ellis Miller, Aberri Olaskoaga, Richard Overstreet, Nicole Parent, Natasha Parry, Irving Penn, Caroline Pinon, Oscar de la Renta, Baronne Alain de Rothschild, Penelope Rowlands, Richard Sieburth, Danielle Slavik, Jean Stein, Susan Train, Florence Van der Kemp, Claudia Verbaum, and Gore Vidal.

And special thanks to Gaël Mamine and the Balenciaga Archives Paris for their patience and generosity.

PERMISSIONS
ACKNOWLEDGMENTS

ILLUSTRATION CREDITS

125	Courtesy of Condé Nast
127	© Irving Penn, Courtesy of Condé Nast
129	Courtesy of Collection Jean-Claude Janet, All Rights Reserved
131	© Bert Stern, Courtesy of Condé Nast
132	© Irving Penn, Courtesy of Condé Nast
133	Courtesy of Balenciaga Archives Paris
134	Courtesy of Balenciaga Archives Paris
137	Courtesy of Balenciaga Archives Paris
138	© Keystone / Hulton Archive / Getty Images
143	© Tom Kublin, Balenciaga Archives Paris
144	© Irving Penn, Courtesy of Condé Nast
145	© Karen Radkai, Courtesy of Condé Nast
148	© Harry Meerson, All Rights Reserved
151	Courtesy of Balenciaga Archives Paris
152	Courtesy of Balenciaga Archives Paris
155	© Tom Kublin, Balenciaga Archives Paris
156	Courtesy of Special Collections, Gladys Marcus Library, Fashion Institute of Technology
157	Courtesy of Balenciaga Archives Paris
159	© Manuel Outumuro, Fundación Cristóbal Balenciaga Fundazioa
161	© Henri Cartier-Bresson, Courtesy of Magnum Photos
164	Courtesy of Collection Florette Chelot, All Rights Reserved
173	Courtesy of Condé Nast
178–79	Courtesy of Air France
181	© Irving Penn, Courtesy of Condé Nast
183	Courtesy of Collection Florette Chelot, All Rights Reserved
184	Courtesy of Balenciaga Archives Paris
192	Courtesy of the author
211	Mona Strader Bismarck Collection, Courtesy of The Filson Historical Society

INSERT

1	© Manuel Outumuro, Fundación Cristóbal Balenciaga Fundazioa
2	© Manuel Outumuro, Fundación Cristóbal Balenciaga Fundazioa
3	© Manuel Outumuro, Fundación Cristóbal Balenciaga Fundazioa
4	Courtesy of Balenciaga Archives Paris
5	© Manuel Outumuro, Fundación Cristóbal Balenciaga Fundazioa
6	© Manuel Outumuro, Fundación Cristóbal Balenciaga Fundazioa
7	© Manuel Outumuro, Fundación Cristóbal Balenciaga Fundazioa
8	© Manuel Outumuro, Fundación Cristóbal Balenciaga Fundazioa

Printed in the USA
CPSIA information can be obtained
at www.ICGtesting.com
LVHW031239260224
772797LV00004B/421